◆ *A Friend in Need (detail) by C.M. Coolidge* ◆

a FRIENDLY game of POKER

52 TAKES on the NEIGHBORHOOD GAME

Edited by Jake Austen

CHICAGO REVIEW PRESS

Library of Congress Cataloging-in-Publication Data

A friendly game of poker : 52 takes on the neighborhood game / edited by
Jake Austen.— 1st ed.
    p. cm.
  ISBN 1-55652-512-5
  1. Poker—Miscellanea. I. Austen, Jake. II. Title.
GV1253.F75 2003
795.41'2—dc21

2003004381

Cover image: *A Friend in Need* by C. M. Coolidge
Cover design: Mel Kupfer
Interior design: Monica Baziuk

Published by Chicago Review Press, Incorporated
814 North Franklin Street
Chicago, Illinois 60610
ISBN 1-55652-512-5
Printed in the United States of America

5   4   3   2   1

To my daughter, Maiya,

although I hope she grows up to have better things to do

with her life than play poker all day.

However, I do expect her to be very good at it.

contents

Table Tales

♣

Practical and Impractical Tips

♣

Poker in Culture

Foreword

OK, LET'S GET THIS OUT OF THE WAY. Gambling is wrong. Hahahahahaha.

Me, the way I do it is, once a week or so, I come home, put on the teev or read a magazine while I play on-line for money for a couple hours.

When I tell friends that I play poker on-line for money they act concerned. Something about it seems seedy to them, and sad. Like: "Don'tcha have something better to do with your time than chase cards with money?" Like: "Don'tcha think things have gotten a little out of hand?"

But if poker's wrong, why does it feel so right? In a way, everything in this book is an answer to that question.

I'm actually playing on-line in a $5 hold 'em tournament at www.pokerroom.com as I write this. Eleven of us are at my table and right now, I'm doing worse than everyone, thanks to an ace-to-five straight of mine that got beaten by some bullshit fours-over-threes full house on the river.

Look at how manly that last sentence looks, sitting there on the page. Honestly, as a person working in public broadcasting, I never get to say anything with that much testosterone coursing through it in my non-poker life. I'm guessing that's true for a number of the contributors in this book. Soft, decent people who write for a living and get to feel tough when they have cards in their hands.

If you want actual information about how to play poker, this isn't the book for you. For that, go to Doyle Brunson's amazing *Super/System*, which has the air of one of those books Hermione and Ron and Harry Potter study at the Hogwarts School, full of very useful and arcane instruction and folk tradition, laid down by those who really know. You can't believe that the card sharks you'd be a fool to play poker with would take the time to sit down and write books full of their secret craft. T. J. Cloutier's and David Sklansky's books are also pretty good. The book you're holding in your hands is better than those in one important respect: it's about poker played by mortals. You and I would have a chance at winning some money at a table with many of these writers.

Hey! Just quadrupled my chips with an ace-king that turned into a pair of kings with an ace kicker, throwing me into second place. Stand back!

Here's another thing. I hate poker. I hate it because in order to play well, you have to fold a lot of hands, which means that there's a lot of sitting on your ass watching other people while you wait for decent cards or a decent bluff. It's very boring. I can't emphasize this enough. I get restless, and invariably end up playing cards I should've folded, simply because I can't stand waiting out another hand. Needless to say, this costs me some money.

But I keep playing. Because the long stretches of boredom are punctuated with moments of real drama. Because every time a card is given to me, every time a card comes down on the table, I feel that little surge of hope. Sure, it's usually quashed, but sometimes it works out. Even better, sometimes I manage to trick people into believing I got the good cards. Either way, it's so thrilling that I don't need it to happen very often to want to come back for more.

I got so caught up in writing those last two paragraphs for you that I've been playing carelessly. Stayed in two different hands I should've folded. And then, with only four players left, about to be blinded out, I played an ace-four and got beat by a spades flush. Thanks a lot. Another five dollars shot to hell and you're to blame. Which is pretty much how it goes for us amateurs. We pay attention to the action, but only to a point. We're disciplined, but only to a point. Aggressive, but only to a point. When we play with friends, if we're lucky, the jokes get better and the poker gets worse as the hours go on. That's the kind of poker this book's about. Home poker. Poker for suckers like you and me.

Ira Glass

Host of public radio's *This American Life*

acknowledgments

THE EDITOR would like to thank his poker buddies and his family (not necessarily in that order) for their support and assistance with this project. The editor also extends his gratitude to the following individuals, without whom this collection would not have been possible: Bob Abrahamian, Benjamin Austen, Ernestine Austen, Ralph Austen, Ken Burke, Greg Dinkin, Barbara Holt, Josh Mills, Jacqueline Stewart, Nikki Stewart, and Yuval Taylor.

INTRODUCTION

by Jake Austen

"THE LIST of now well-established oxymorons," wrote Joseph Epstein in *The New Yorker*, "should, I believe, be expanded to include 'friendly poker game.' There is no such thing as a friendly poker game."

The problem with Epstein's logic is that he has an idealistic definition of the "friend" in "friendship." In reality, friendship is a complex experience, and there is poetic beauty in the ways real-life camaraderie balances people's worst character flaws with the social obligations of being buddies. There's no better place to explore this precarious balance than at the poker table. The neighborhood poker game certainly isn't the only place where "friends" tell lies to, take advantage of, and siphon money from their chums, but it may be the only place where five minutes later the deceptions are revealed, owned up to, accepted, and, ultimately, admired. Poker among pals might be the site of some of the most honest interactions men experience as they share intense, dramatic, intimate showdowns. Compared with the sterile encounter of challenging strangers and a dealer in a casino, these are profoundly more meaningful (and fun) experiences.

While legalized gambling, semilegal poker clubs, and interest in poker in general have all grown over the last decade, the weekly, casual, amateur poker game between friends has always flourished as a cherished part of American culture. The ritual of getting together with cohorts and playing archaic, dramatic parlor games into the wee hours of the night is arguably our country's number-one participant sport. For those engaged in the more serious, expensive home games, this really can be a sport where the purse is everything. But for most players a weekly game is an escape, a safe place to engage in the fantasies poker allows. Those fantasies can be as profound as imagining we are all heirs to the legacy of poker "cool," each of us a cowboy, a mobster, a riverboat gambler when we have our cards on the table. Those fantasies can be as boorish as imagining we are still young enough to stay up past twelve on a weeknight. The important thing is that, unlike the fantasies of the armchair quarterback, the poker player is really in the game. The game may involve nickels, but it is "the game" nonetheless.

Defining "friendly" or "home" or "neighborhood poker" is not really necessary, as the parameters change from game to game. A one-dollar win at a table of janitors can be the equivalent of a $200 win at a table of surgeons. Friendly poker cannot even be defined by its atmosphere. While home poker has traditionally embraced obtuse rules and silly games, the popularity of Texas hold 'em has narrowed the gap between the vibes of home and casino poker. In the film *It's a Wonderful Life*, Nick the bartender tells Clarence the bumbling angel, "We serve hard drinks in here for men who want to get drunk fast, and we don't need characters around to give the joint atmosphere." Texas hold 'em is hard drinks for serious poker players. Anaconda, southern cross, auction, Dr. Pepper—these are the "mulled wine, heavy on the cinnamon, light on the cloves" of poker. But in the end, friendly poker is not about what games you play. Whether you embrace the serious or the silly side, it is the social experiences that are the heart of home poker. And they are experiences that invite literary reflection.

This book features essays by a diverse group of writers on the joys, regrets, friendships, philosophies, and adventures that they have experienced through home poker. It features a section of appropriately unhelpful hints to apply to your home game, a game for which you and your table mates should be the ultimate authority. It also features a studious section on poker as it has been documented in culture. This cornucopia of fascinating facts about poker paintings, poker movies, poker books, and other card-themed masterpieces can be used to liven up conversation between bets (or as a distraction when you don't want your opponents to notice your mighty hand developing). Within these pages, issues as important as gender, race, and mortality are covered. But they are given no more weight than issues of folding, checking, and raising.

It is unlikely that anything in this book will lead you to riches. One hopes there is nothing in here that will send you to the poorhouse. In the end, this book probably won't make you a better player. But hopefully, it captures what it feels like to hang out half the night, drinking beer and playing pasteboards with your cronies with far more clarity (and joy) than a formal poker guide ever could.

Pinched with Four Aces by C.M. Coolidge

TABLE TALES

a Hand for the ages

by Greg Dinkin

IT'S 1:00 A.M., which wouldn't be such a big deal had you not told your woman that you'd be home by midnight. Forget that it's a Wednesday night and you have to give a presentation at 8:00 A.M. You're losing—$80 and a whole lot of pride.

The game is five-card draw and you're dealt a pair of aces, a pair of threes, and a deuce. The maximum bet before the draw is $2, and you keep your snicker to yourself as Louie, the player to your left, bets. Including you, there are six players in the game, and everyone calls except Ron, the resident tightwad.

When Louie draws three cards, you know that he has only a pair and isn't much of a threat. Two other players do the same before Mo knuckles the table. Wow, he's standing pat, which you know means that he's either bluffing or has a made hand—at worst a straight. You draw one, but can't bear to look.

Louie is first to act and checks. The next two players also check before it gets to Mo, who checks as well. Suddenly, it's your turn to act, but before you do, you try to figure out why Mo checked. Because you raised before the draw, he may be sandbagging. The old check-raise is Mo's forte.

You finally decide to look at the card you drew. But you don't just look at it, you have to squeeeeeze it, not so much to add to the drama,

3

but because you are terrified to look. As you start to squeeze, you see nothing but white space. Could it be the A?

As Marv Albert would say: Yes!

You bet $5. Louie folds, as do the next two players, and it's up to Mo. "Make it ten," he says, check-raising, just as you thought. But this time you have aces full—time to show that sandbagger.

"I'll see it and raise you five more," you say. The pot has grown to more than fifty bucks, not to mention the five more you'll get when Mo calls your raise. But he doesn't comply. Instead, he raises again.

Up until this point, you assumed that he had been dealt a made hand, such as a straight or a flush. Since the odds are 693 to 1 that he was dealt a full house, you figure that's unlikely, and even if he had it, it wouldn't beat your aces full. But wait a second. Mo is no dummy, and he has to know that you wouldn't keep raising without a big hand. So the question is: What does he think you have?

Since you drew one card, he may think you made a straight or a flush. But he's also smart enough to know that you're not the type of player who raises before the draw on the come. So, he had to figure you for having two pair. And after your reraise after the draw, he now has to believe that you made your full house. So why is he still raising?

It may be because he thinks he has a big full house, such as kings full. You raise again. Without even hesitating, Mo says, "Make it $30." The good news is that there's now more than $80 in the pot. The bad news is that you know that Mo knows that you have a full house, and he keeps raising. You stop to think again.

The odds of Mo being dealt four of a kind are 4,164 to 1, and besides, you know him well enough to know that if he were dealt four of a kind, he would have drawn a card, just to make his hand look less intimidating. So you rule that out, and raise again.

"Make it $40," says Mo.

Now you're all but convinced that he was dealt a straight flush. Since you can't win the pot, you decide to come up with Plan B.

"Hey, Ron," you say to the tightwad, who is a professional statistician. "What are the odds of being dealt a straight flush on the first five cards?"

"64,973 to 1," says Ron.

"Are you kiddin' me?" says Louie, who you're not even sure can count that high. "How many zeros is that?"

"Make it two zeros," you say to Louie. "I'll bet you 100 to 1 that he's got a straight flush—my buck to your C-note."

"I've been playing poker twenty years," says Louie, "and I ain't never seen no one dealt a straight flush right off the deal. You're on."

When you ask Mo to turn over his hand, he says, "Not until you see the bet."

So now it's going to cost you another five bucks to see the hand, bringing the total pot to more than $100. As far as you're concerned, the drama is over. If he's got the straight flush, you win $100 from Louie. If he doesn't, you win the $100 in the pot.

You throw in the five bucks, quite proud of yourself for putting together this remarkable hedge. Mo, perhaps to add drama to this little affair, or maybe because he's always loved to jerk you around, decides that he'll turn his cards over one at a time.

The first card is the K of hearts; next is the K of diamonds.

"Pay up," screams Louie, and you gladly throw him a buck; 64,973 to 1 shots don't come in that often. When the third card he turns over is the K of clubs, followed by the ten of spades, you start kicking yourself for not having raised him more.

"I thought you might have had kings full," you say, as you show him your aces full. "If you'd had the four of a kind, you wouldn't have stood pat."

"Nice read," Mo says, as he turns over his fifth and final card—the K of spades.

♣

a Wasted Evening

by Ashley Adams

I'M ALWAYS LOOKING for a poker game. My rule is that I'll play in any game I can find, if I can afford it. No matter how bad the game seems to be at first, I've found that there is always something redeeming about it.

My convictions were tested on a Tuesday night in Boston about ten years ago. I had accepted an invitation from the eighty-year-old former president of my synagogue to play in his weekly poker game. He was a World War II veteran, long since retired from the clothing business. He'd had this game for over fifty years with the same bunch of GI buddies of his, most of whom were still members of the temple. One of them had recently died, so he was trying to fill his slot by inviting me. It was an interesting group of guys—all retired, all veterans, and all white-haired, genteel gentlemen.

Here was the setup. Everyone arrived at 7:00 P.M. sharp with their wives. There were five to ten minutes of hellos and kisses while the wives organized for a night out and the guys got settled in. As soon as the wives had left, the guys got out the cards and started to play, and a half-century of age seemed to lift from them. Their language got a bit spicy, reminiscent of life in the barracks or on the battlefield. For me, a young pup of forty, it was funny to hear these elderly gentlemen throwing around the "f" and "s" words so casually. But for them, I suppose, it was a reminder that they were just the guys without their wives and that they could say and do as they pleased—even if that included gambling and cursing.

Anyone who claims that poker is just about the money has not spent any time in games like this one. The game was seven-card stud. Everyone anted twenty-five cents. The betting limit was five cents until a pair showed or until the last card was dealt. Then it went to ten cents. That was it. A twenty-five-cent ante and no more than a ten-cent bet. One raise was allowed per round.

They never covered this kind of a game in any of the poker books I had read!

Though I was a pretty experienced poker player, I was not an experienced enough person to appreciate the game for what it really was. I took it seriously as a contest. In my head, the goal for the night would be to win as much money as I could even with this offbeat structure. I said to myself that the absolute amount of money won or lost was irrelevant. It was how many bets an hour that was important. I quickly figured out that if winning $40 in a four-hour five-to-ten-dollar game was a decent win, then in this game $4 should be my goal. I told myself that a good poker player would be able to devise a winning strategy no matter what the stakes or the structure.

So I decided to size up the players, think about the structure, and figure out a way to win. The players were all loose-passive. This means that they pretty much just called every bet. And every bet was five cents, unless on the last card a player had a great hand, in which case he bet ten cents. I decided the best I could do was to play aggressively early on to build the pots when I had a high pair or even a very strong drawing hand, like three suited cards headed by an ace.

Their congeniality and friendship seemed to get in the way of my mission. Rather than play continuously for the four hours they had allotted for the poker game, they took a break in the middle of play. At 9:00 P.M. sharp, the players got out a coffee cake brought by one of the wives and had a twenty-minute break—with coffee and tea. I was pleasant but clearly impatient, eager to get back in the game.

I didn't engage much in the chitchat, lest I prolong the break in the action.

We reconvened at precisely 9:20. It was more of the same poker. I was loose and aggressive up front and tight and passive later on. I figured that a nickel saved was a nickel earned. There was also no point in bluffing, as everyone called everything. Pot odds occasionally had me drawing to long shots. But when they didn't come in, I'd fold (unlike nearly everyone else at the table).

My strategy seemed to pay off. I was ahead $4.15 by the end of the night. Though I could have won one hundred times that much if I had gone to the poker room at the nearby Foxwoods Casino, I still congratulated myself for achieving my goal for the night, pleased that I had won over forty big bets for the evening.

Then, at precisely 11:00 P.M., the host announced, "Last hand, guys!" Everyone reached into their wallets and threw $5 in the pot!!!

The dealer then dealt out five up cards to each player. The winning hand won the pot of $40. I lost. I went from being a $4.15 winner to being an eighty-five-cent loser. All because of some ridiculous game of $5 showdown!

At first I was angry. I had spent the whole night devising a winning strategy and capitalizing on it, only to have it all thrown out the window with some absurd crapshoot.

"What a waste!" I silently thought to myself as I drove home.

A few months later, two of the guys in the game died. One year later, the host died, and the game came to an end. I went to sit shiva in the house where I had played poker a year earlier with Arthur and his army buddies. I met his widow, his children, and some of the widows of his buddies. I heard them talk about this game and the other activities that they had shared for fifty years. I realized what a wonderful thing this game really was for these gentlemen, how it had kept them together as friends for half a century. And I thought about my behavior during the one evening when they had given me an opportunity to share it.

"What a waste," I silently thought to myself as I drove home.

He WHO Steals MY Purse ain't no Friend of Mine

by Nick Tosches

I'M LISTENING TO A SONG called "Billy & Oscar," written by my old friend Dave Hickey, and recorded by my old friend Jim Dickinson on his album *Free Beer Tomorrow*. The song is a beautifully imagined danse macabre about Billy the Kid (1859–81) and Oscar Wilde (1854–1900), and it contains the lines:

> There's more to the journey than the distance traversed,
> And the price of the ticket comes out of the purse.

Yes, indeed, the price of the ticket comes out of the purse. Nobody wins. And yet the purse, ever to be slit by fate, again and again, is what lures us on.

The purse, the purse, the purse—metaphorically and truly—it all comes down to the purse.

Let us tell now of the cards and the purse, and the notion of their being encircled by false friends or worse.

There is no such thing as a friendly poker game—not as long as there is a purse to be taken. When one plays poker, one is out to drink the blood of those with whom one plays. Friends do not desire to

defeat or take money from one another. A game of poker is a pro-
longed act of vicious deceit and greed on the part of every player,
directed against every other player. Poker is a game in which all players must be enemies. The nature of the game demands it. Poker cannot be played among friends, but only among those who call
themselves friends. To play poker according to the enduring principles of Cicero's *De Amicitia* is to lose. "Friendly poker" is an oxy-
moron in the extreme.

I recall an illuminating evening of more than twenty years ago.
Sitting or lying on my floor were: Lester Bangs, who then still was
not technically deceased; Mike McGovern, a crime reporter who also
had been something of a professional poker player back in his home-
town of Chicago; and myself. With us was a pint of Monastery-
brand grain alcohol, which was also from Chicago, and a deck of
cards. We had embarked on a game of small-stakes "friendly poker."
Of course, small stakes often escalate, as ten-cent bets become two-
bit bets and two-bit bets become dollar bets. Just as he was running
out of money, Lester was dealt five cards that he was sure could not
be beaten. He bemoaned his fate that he did not have the money to
raise the stake substantially. At this point I had already folded my
hand.

"How much do you want to raise?" Mike asked him.

"At least ten bucks, if I had it," Lester said.

"Here," said Mike, reaching into his pocket, withdrawing a ten-
dollar bill, and passing it to Lester. "I'll lend it to you."

Lester thanked him and laid down the ten.

How much friendlier could a friendly game be?

Mike looked at Lester.

"I see the ten and raise you twenty," he said.

And that was that. Mike scooped up all the coins and bills that
were on the floor.

"Don't forget," he said to Lester, whose mouth was agape in hay-
seed bafflement: "you owe me ten."

This was friendly poker in its truest essence. Imagine what the game might have been if only we'd had the money to be *really* friendly.

Friends. Poker friends. They're everywhere. Consider the deep and bittersweet resonance in the words by which mafiosi often refer to their own kind: *gli amici degli amici*—the friends of friends.

LADY LUCK, MAKE ME A MAN

by Benjamin Austen

"There lurks, perhaps, in every human heart a desire of distinction,
which inclines every man to hope, and then to believe, that nature
has given himself something peculiar unto himself."
— SAMUEL JOHNSON

"I'll take one."
— ME, going for an inside straight at five-card draw

WHEN IT'S MY DEAL and my turn to call the game, I ask the men around the table, friends and friends of friends, if they know of any poker good-luck charms. "I make sure I'm playing with you," Mustafa, who recently changed his name from Floyd, tells me. "I always wear my special red-and-white thong panties," Doug says. John chips in, "I let my balls hang out of my shorts and fondle them before touching the cards." This is a friendly game, a bimonthly gathering of quarter-ante, four-dollar-maximum-raise poker. No diamond-encrusted horseshoe pinky rings; no orange-haired trolls, alligator's teeth, or mojo bags. None of us wears sunglasses. Khalil responds to the question by throwing five dollars in front of me. "Here's your luck," he says. "Cut the deck. High card wins."

I don't take his bet. I avoid games of excessive chance, believing they can't discriminate between the merely lucky and the truly deserving. Instead I deal seven-card stud, nothing wild, and wait for everyone else to touch their hands before I touch mine. Doug is slow peeking at his two down cards, so I have to bet blind the first round. Then I surreptitiously graze the knuckle of my right thumb against the marble-sized, wooden baseball I wear around my neck and hidden underneath my shirt, rap my cards twice, mouthing, "Hook me up, Dave" (something I've been saying since it first brought me luck fifteen years earlier), and assess my hand. Queen and nine in the hole. A four showing. A rainbow of three suits.

I'm not completely alone in my courting of good fortune. John sports a straw cowboy hat most nights we play. I notice that Doug lays his unclasped watch alongside rows of neatly stacked, color-coordinated chips. After Mustafa shows us pictures from a trip he and his family took to Egypt, he leaves on the table a single photograph of himself and Mustafa, Jr., standing in front of the pyramids. Khalil bets wildly, winning and losing big, challenging us to side bets and haranguing us regardless of his success. Having known me the longest, he theatrically shouts "Hook me up, Dave" as he draws cards. After the fourth time Mustafa "forgets" to ante, Khalil reminds him, calling him Floyd and quickly being corrected. "I knew you back in college when you were just Floyd," Khalil says, "and that's what I'm gonna call you. Throw in a quarter, Floyd."

I've always taken my poker with talisman and ritual, and been a little bit embarrassed by this. In high school I declared an unexceptional rock to be magic and conspicuously brought it to poker games in a jewelry case with all the irony and mock-affectedness of a teenager manufacturing distinction. Still, I wouldn't let others touch it and I didn't play without it. I also buried amid my stake a lucky red-faced quarter, a coin I colored myself with magic marker. For several years I sat at poker tables wearing a White Sox cap with the baseball card of my favorite player glued into the inside lining. One year in college I ate pickled kumquats before every poker game.

As I've played poker, I've tested these objects and customs, secretly wishing to stumble upon the one that would charm my life, or, rather, prove I was already charmed. My conception of luck is much like the early Protestant notion of material wealth: it's a consequence of one's election and worth, not the cause. A string of luck, then, means you aren't simply luckier than the other guys at the table; you are somehow more capable. And if you've consistently done your part—brought the talisman, carried out the rituals, avoided the jinxes—then you are that much more deserving.

While the Protestants had that "ethic" thing and worked like ants, I've never read a poker book, mastered the art of betting, or paid enough attention to my opponents or their cards. Consequently, I generally lose at poker. Those who consistently come out ahead do so by playing good hands and not playing weak hands, but I don't know when to fold 'em. I'm too eager to explore the mysteries of the deck, to discover where a game will lead me. Lady Luck, reveal to me the kind of man I dream I am. Pick me, not him.

I dislike games with shared or rotating cards, so when Mustafa deals a Texas hold 'em I go get beer. Literally and metaphorically, I want to play the hand I am dealt. When I return, John's wife, Vera, is sitting by her husband. She studies the table and John's cards and consults with him on his choices. In a game of seven-card stud, I ride a pair of fours, keeping the betting as light as possible, waiting for the deck to deliver a winning hand. And the deck delivers. My seventh card, the queen of diamonds, transforms my low pair into a flush. I open the betting and then stay in even after Doug and John start raising one another the four-dollar maximum. Only after my flush loses to Doug's full house, which loses to John's better full house, do I realize that everyone but me knew I didn't have the winning hand. John rakes in the pot with the V of his bent arm. Vera says, "See, I'm good luck, honey."

At the age of nine, I anxiously awaited puberty, hoping, among other things, to find that I possessed the powers of a superhero. According to Marvel Comics, puberty was the moment when your superpowers emerged. As foolish as it was, this bit of childhood fancy was not so different from the clichés that had been driven into me about becoming anything I wanted, if only I put my mind to it. On the contrary, adulthood seems like a constant discovery of limitations, a whittling away at the myths of one's own election. One forms like some plants do, hitting a ceiling and branching off in different directions. In almost everything I do, I am a man of diligence and logic. At poker, however, I believe in luck, chance, and the insights they provide. While I'm playing, I imagine limitless possibilities. I'm like the guys who instinctively look under the hood of a woman's stalled car, even though they've never even done an oil change. By looking, I think, maybe I'll reveal some manly knowledge, some innate ability, I didn't even know I had.

I'm down to a few dollars in chips, and I consider cashing in and driving home. But I buy in with my last ten dollars, taking the chips from John's winnings rather than the bank. I rap my cards; I hang the wooden baseball outside my shirt; I say out loud, "Hook me up, Dave." I am dealt ten, jack, queen, all in spades. I think my luck can change, and I play on.

mr. vegas

by Nolan Dalla

B EFORE PURSUING life as a writer and professional gambler, I
took my first real "nine-to-five" job working as an insurance
salesman. What a dreadful job that was. I rented an apartment outside of Dallas, and began dressing the part of Marlin Perkins. One
thing I quickly learned about the insurance business is that a significant part of my "training" would include drinking and gambling
with my colleagues. Forget the image of insurance agents as boring,
conservative types. What I remember is barstools, strip clubs, and
regular visits to Vegas. One salesman in his forties supervised my
development. His name was Justin.

Justin had previously lived in Las Vegas for several years, and had
done a stint as a blackjack dealer. This made him something of a
celebrity among the other insurance agents, who all looked to Justin
as the office playboy. Since Justin always wore silk shirts and flashy
clothes, everyone in the office called him "Mr. Vegas." Between sales
calls, most of our time was spent reading the *Racing Form*, handi-
capping the day's sporting events, or playing gin rummy. Insurance
policies—are you kidding? So much for us being "the good-hands
people." The only good hands we were concerned with were of the
five-card variety.

Justin's real love was poker. The problem was we couldn't get enough players for a weekly poker game. The answer to our prayers came when a pool party was scheduled at my apartment complex. Plenty of free booze and loose money floating around made it seem like the perfect opportunity for a poker game. Everyone expected Justin, the poker expert, to win big.

That Friday night, we put all the furniture into the back room and set up a poker table. The game started. Within an hour the place was absolute bedlam, with dozens of people strolling in and out, and a long waiting list. Unfortunately, Justin didn't seem to be doing particularly well. We played the normal games—stud, draw, and hold 'em—but Justin kept right on losing his money. To add insult to injury, kids in wet bathing suits who were either too drunk or too stoned to know that a flush beat a straight put bad beat after bad beat on the silk-shirted Justin. Mr. Vegas just couldn't manage to win a hand. Then he went on massive tilt. Pretty soon it became obvious that Justin wasn't nearly as good as we figured.

Maybe the cards were running bad for Justin that night. But I doubt it. Within a year, Justin left the insurance business and owed local bookies so much money that he skipped town.

LiTTLe LUCKY

FranceS FoSTer recallS Poker
On THe SOUTH SIDe OF CHICago In THe 1940S

by James Porter

*Frances Foster is a petite, eighty-two-year-old lady who has long
been a friend of my family. With her, poker wasn't just a card
game, it was an entire lifestyle. Chicago's African American community has long been a stronghold for bid-whist games, but half
a century ago poker held its own. Though she long ago forsook
poker for casino blackjack, she remembers that era as if it happened a half-hour ago. This is how Ms. Foster told it.*

H OW I GOT STARTED WAS, we lived above a store, and this little lady had a group downstairs, she had a little Po-Ke-No
game. We were playing for pennies and I kind of liked it, but I wanted
to learn poker so badly. My husband and I were rooming at a place
and this man said he would teach me to play poker, so I graduated
from Po-Ke-No to playing poker. This was in the 1940s—I learned
how to play in 1941 and then I played until 1946.

I was very lucky at first and I was winning every time I'd go. They
called me Little Lucky.

I played with people I knew; I didn't play strangers. I belonged to a little poker club. Every night I would go play with somebody and then on the next week I would have my game, so everybody I'd gone to, they came to my game then. We'd sell food [to the players who came to games we hosted]—I think in those days we were getting seventy-five cents for a dinner. We'd have fried chicken and we'd have steak and we'd have ribs. Sometimes we'd have a boiled dinner.

I was the baby of the bunch, but I was a very good poker player. If you had a jack up and I had less than a queen as my hole card I wouldn't play the hand. I picked my toughest player and I played a card over him all the time. I didn't have to have a pair to start out with. One time, I will never forget, I was at the 411, a little tavern at 411 East 63rd Street. They had a little hotel upstairs and we used to play cards up there. We'd ante, first fifty cents, then when we looked at our first card we'd put a dollar in as a blind. One time I was playing with this electrician, and do you know I called a blind with a six down. I don't know what made me do it. And bam here comes a six, made me have a pair of sixes. I'll never forget that day. I had about $75 in front of me, and that man said, "Take all or nothing, I'm going to bet it all." So he bet all the rest of my $75. So I had a jack on my hand. So he said, "Well I got a king on my hand, I got an ace-king." So he went to take the pot, I said, "Wait a minute, I have a pair of sixes." He said, "Aw dogdarnit, how did you call on that?" To this day I don't know what made me call on that six. And then I quit playing for the day, came on home.

Then in 1946 I had a friend, he was going to San Francisco. He said, "Listen, I want to show you something . . . I'm going to show you what I'm going to put on the cards." It was silver, it came in a little container and he wiped his fingers on it and marked the kings, the queens, and the jacks. And so he said, "I'll riffle the deck and I'm going to throw the cards out and I want you to pick out the kings and the queens and the jacks." The kings, they were marked at the short end and the jacks were at the corner and blah blah blah . . . So anyway, that's when I thought about stopping. Anytime a person shows me where he's going to put the stuff and I can't see it I don't need to play cards anymore.

It was also getting dangerous. A couple of insurance agents, they were supposed to be insurance agents, they came to our game and they were marking the cards, and that kind of broke things up. One of our players, Youngblood, he owned about three pool halls on the South Side . . . he was tall and light and had nice hair. . . . He said, "Man, you're cheating!" He brought it to their attention, and that's when the big thing ensued . . . it was a big ruckus! And when the ruckus started they knocked the table over, so all the money fell on the floor. So I picked up the money, the big bills, and I stuck it in my pocket book and I ran up the stairs. There was a fellow that was there and he said [whispering], "Hand me the money, they won't take it from me." So I handed him the money, but I left some in my hand-bag. When you're gambling you carry the big bills at the bottom and the small bills at the top. So when the money fell it fell *over*, so when I handed the man the money I handed him the big bills. When I got home I only had twenty-six singles.

I played poker from 1941 until about 1946 and that's when the insurance men broke up the game. Then I said, "I don't need to be going to the game. It's getting too dangerous now."

Then I graduated from that and I started working at a racehorse bookie. Harry Fields had a racehorse bookie on 41st Street. So every day at two o'clock when my husband would go to work I would go to the bookie. The bookie had made money all the morning, and when I came they used to say, "Little Lucky, who's the winner?" I'd say, "Well, look at 518 without a call, that's the winner today." So I'd bet me a little dollar on it. So Harry Fields told me, "Listen, every day we make some money until you come. I'm going to get you a job writing tickets at the racehorse book. *But you can't bet.*"

They called me Little Lucky.

WHAT ABOUT POKER?

by Thomas Edward Shaw

O UR RULES WERE SIMPLE. When it's your turn to deal, you get to name the game—five-card draw, five-card stud, or seven-card stud. We only played for nickels and the game was always at Mark Brunner's trailer house.

Brunner was the banker because he had a large bowl filled with nickels. He also had the nicest car in town: a 1958 Chevy convertible. It was light blue and had a continental spare-tire kit on the trunk. All the girls wanted to ride in it. Brunner lived a couple of blocks away from the whorehouses.

Elko, Nevada, had five whorehouses. Ida's was the most popular. If you listen to what everyone says, Ida could have been elected mayor if she wanted. The locals still talk about the time she got sick and went to the hospital and everyone in town came to visit. Her room was so filled with flowers, there was hardly enough room for anyone to sit down.

We played poker at least one night a week. Usually there were five of us. We barely fit inside of Brunner's trailer, the table right in front of the door. To get a beer, you only had to stand up, squeeze past a chair or two, and reach over to the refrigerator that never had any food in it. The game would go on without interruption.

I had just graduated from high school in Carson City. I was in Elko to work on a survey crew for the summer. Back then, Elko was a quiet cow town. It was on the Southern and Western Pacific Railroad line and many of the locals worked for the railroad. Brunner was one of them.

He was a tall guy with dark hair, always dressed neatly. He had a dry sense of humor and for him the game was never anything more than a way to pass the evening.

The person sitting to his left, Lee Hart, worked on the same survey crew I did. He had a tendency to whine, and usually whatever he wanted he never got. He liked the girls but they never liked him. When it came to poker, Lee Hart was a purist. He refused to believe that anything other than five-card draw, nothing wild, was poker.

The person next to him was Ken Davis, a very rational guy with thick glasses and a somewhat intellectual look. He always tried to identify things for what they were. For him, poker was nothing more than playing the cards you're dealt. Doing anything else was wasted effort. His goal was to become a civil engineer. He was as smart and honest as anyone can get in Elko. If he had to bluff, his truthfulness could work against him. But he won his share of hands. Not always big pots, mind you, but enough to at least break even. There are people who play the game one unit at a time, always steady, always taking as long as they need to get ahead.

Me, I lose patience. I always feel as if I'm on the edge of an abyss. I'm not sure I like poker, but I play it. It's like life. Life is unfair. Life is a gamble. If life is going to be good, I win the hand. If I'm going to have a bad year, or be carried away on the road to perdition, I'll lose the hand. Yes, I played poker.

Next to me was Glen Roylance, a small guy with just the slightest hint of an impish grin on his pimple-covered face. Roylance was quite different from me—he always went for broke. If he couldn't win with the cards he was dealt, then he'd try to lie his way through—

or at least make it impossible for the rest of us to feel confident about our hands. For him, poker was a test of strength.

◆

"OK, Roylance, it's your deal." Brunner passed the deck.

Roylance looked around the table, smiled, and began to shuffle. "We're gonna play seven-card stud, one-eyed jacks are wild, and so are women with tits."

It always got a reaction from Hart. "All of 'em?" he asked.

"Yep."

"That's way too many wild cards, Roylance. . . . "

"That's what makes it exciting!"

"That ain't poker. With so many wild cards, it's impossible to figure out how to bet."

"It's my deal. I'll call what I want."

Roylance shuffled the deck. The person to his right—me—cut. Roylance dealt the first two cards face down, and started dealing the third card face up.

A card flew to Brunner. Roylance spoke as he dealt. "A ten. Anything's possible."

As the host and banker, Brunner didn't really care. "Does anyone want a beer?" he asked.

Roylance tossed a card to Hart. "A deuce. Better have something underneath."

Hart peeked under his cards and groaned.

The next card was dealt to Davis. "Another deuce. You and Hart are tied."

Davis lifted his hole cards ever so slightly to take a peek, then softly laid them back down, revealing no expression.

"Eddie, you got an ace. You're high man on the table."

My future was looking up. I had one wild card in the hole and this ace was a good way to begin. I shook my head, then realized I was sending signals. I put on my stone face.

Roylance then dealt to himself. "Ahh, two tits—a wild one. Not bad, not bad. You're high man, Eddie. What's the bet?"

I thought for a moment then realized there was nothing to think about. I pushed a nickel in the pot.

Roylance immediately raised. "I'll see you one nickel and I'll raise one." He always did this—take control of the game when I'm the one with the high card. I threw another nickel in the pot.

"I'm in." Brunner pushed two nickels to the center of the table. "Hart?"

Hart studied his cards and then slowly pushed his two nickels into the pot. He seemed pained. From the looks of it, he didn't have anything, but it was too early to drop out.

Davis was next. He purposefully put his nickels in the pot.

Roylance dealt the next card. "Another ten. You could have four tens—maybe five."

Brunner didn't care. "Tens are nothing in this game."

Roylance continued dealing. "A jack, but it ain't one-eyed . . . and you, Davis, a five, don't mean a thing . . . a nine, Eddie, not much help there." Then he laid the next card on his pile. "By God, a one-eyed jack. I got two wild ones, my ladies. You know this is gonna cost you, don't you?"

Someone got up and grabbed a beer from the refrigerator. Chairs momentarily scraped on the floor. Brunner's two tens was the highest hand. He bet a nickel and it went around the table, everyone contributing their five cents. When it got to Roylance, he paid the nickel and then raised the bet by two more. Everyone mumbled but stayed in, each player shoving two more nickels to the center of the table. By now there had to be $1.50 in the pot. In nickels! And with three more cards to be dealt. Roylance always did this.

Hart complained. "This is supposed to be for fun, Roylance."

"It is fun, Hart. You either play your hand or get out."

"Just 'cause you got a couple of wild cards, Roylance. I think you're trying to buy the pot."

Roylance followed with all the clichés he knew. "The only way to know for sure is put your money where your mouth is. We're all gonna die. Live it up while you can."

Hart rubbed the stubble on his chin and rolled his eyes.

By the time the last bet was made, there was $7.20 in the pot. Normally a pot never goes higher than two or three dollars. Hart folded his cards on the fifth draw. I folded on the sixth. In this game—with so many wild cards—four aces might not mean anything.

"OK, boys, I got three kings. Two wild cards and a king. I was goin' for a royal flush, but it didn't happen."

"You gotta be kiddin'," Hart says. "I had you beat when I folded. I had four deuces."

"You didn't pay to stay."

To my surprise, I had beat him with four aces. What was I thinking? I nodded my head, knowing I had been defeated by fear. Roylance could be one deceptive dude.

Davis won by remaining cool. Nickels are only units of measurement. He figured he had the cards and the nickels to win, and he was right—five fives.

It was my deal next. I went back to five-card draw.

The game always settled down until the deal got back to Roylance. Then he would insist on a whole bunch of wild cards, just to make the game "exciting."

◆

Poker is what we did when there was nothing else to do. We were not old men who needed an escape from pressure. We were young men who needed an escape from boredom. Nights could be slow in Elko. Maybe afterward we might leave Mark's trailer and go to the whorehouse. We were all normal young men from a normal, conservative, small Nevada town.

Looking back on it years later, I wonder if poker had any later effect on our lives. Did we learn anything from it? It's been years since I've read those pages of the devil, and now that I think about it, I have a suspicion that what you read is what you are.

Brunner stayed in Elko, where he worked for the Southern and Western Pacific Railroad. I don't know if he got married or had kids. Someone told me he had a good life.

Hart unhappily worked for the highway department until he quit and then disappeared. Nobody's seen him in years. In a way, he lived the way he played poker—not making the bet.

Davis became the civil engineer he wanted to be. He helped build some impressive highways. He was the main engineer of the four-lane highway that goes up to Lake Tahoe from Carson City. He always measured things one unit at a time.

And me? I became a musician, where I learned that people are formed by the instruments they play. I spent years on the road, where I was dealt some good hands and I was dealt some bad. You can't bluff when you're playing music—and the odds are against you. I did it anyway.

Roylance went to college. After college he was recruited by the CIA. I heard some stories about him in Vietnam. Nothing bad, if you happened to like the war. You hear the stories, and all you can say is, "That's Roylance." I always have to laugh, wondering if the CIA is filled with guys like him. He ended up in Australia, where, someone said, he got married and settled down.

But I digress. About poker, I can only speak for myself. What I learned from playing it is that some people can lie, just naturally—ain't nothin' to it. And others can't help but tell the truth.

How any one of them bets, though, is another matter. It's the bet that counts. If you want to win anything, you first gotta make the bet.

JOHNNY CARSON
AND THE GOURMET POKER CLUB

by Bill Zehme

WHEN A FAMOUS MAN fades from view, you presume dark reasons for such. You gather that grave illness has befallen him. You suspect he is no longer who he was and therefore wishes to enshroud that which he has become in secrecy. Those who know Johnny Carson know better. Even when he was on view regularly, he was barely seen anywhere other than on television screens. His gift for hiding in plain sight has never diminished. Nonetheless, when his heart was refurbished by sudden necessity (via quadruple bypass) three years ago, widespread speculation concluded that health had been the cause of his invisibility all along. His friends, on the other hand, shared a much different reaction. Said television producer George Schlatter, who had been whale-watching with Carson two weeks before the operation: "I didn't know whether it was for real or whether he was just trying to get out of going to a party."

Parties, absolutely, have forever been his scourge. If forced to attend any gathering, he is usually seen in a corner performing sleight-of-hand with quarters. But since he is rarely present in sizeable company, his profile stays near subterranean. "He's great with ten million people; he's not great with ten," says the ever gregarious

Ed McMahon. "He can handle three or four, but ten gets a little pressed for him." ("Ed's always been a guy who thrives on social contact," Carson will note. "I'm just the opposite in personality, you know.") But there is one exception he makes gladly, and that is for the occasional convergences of the Gourmet Poker Club, a kibbitz klatch of exalted show-business pedigree. Besides himself, the membership includes only seven others: Steve Martin, Carl Reiner, Neil Simon, Chevy Chase, mogul Barry Diller, and producers David Chasman and Dan Melnick, the latter of whom originated the game in New York during the 1960s and began hosting it in his Beverly Hills home in the early 1970s. (Because Melnick employed a sublime personal chef, the club earned its gustatory moniker.) When games occur, which is barely more than six times in a year, they occur always on Wednesday nights at 7:30, with dinner served at 9:00, then back to the table until after 11:00. They sit and bet and needle as a circular Rushmore. Chase recalls a night when a delivery guy walked into the room and beheld the assemblage: "The look on his face was utterly gorgeous, like he had seen a poster that had come to life, that couldn't possibly be real. He had to put it out of his mind right away or he was going to wet himself."

"It's the most feminine game in the history of cards," says Martin, who took over hosting chores from Melnick. ("I'm the low-fat host," he asserts.) "It's really about socializing and eating. We're exhausted by 10:30." Says Reiner, "Actually, the card game becomes secondary the minute somebody has a good story to tell. There's a lot of 'Come on, fellas, let's get back to the cards!'" As women have never been welcome at the table, Chasman notes, "We refer to it as our only homosexual pursuit. The remarks uttered throughout are usually very, very sharp. But then the game is conducted under the seal of a confessional." (Chasman designed the club logo—a king of clubs wearing a toque—which has been affixed to baseball caps, sweatshirts, coffee mugs, blazer pins, and the like.) At the most recent game, held February 13, Tom Hanks came to play backup chair and, as with all guest backups, he was given the coffee mug stenciled THE PIGEON. (According to Melnick, by the way, "Johnny won't show up if he knows there's going to be more than one outsider at the table.")

As for the poker-night proclivities of member Carson, member Chase says: "He folds and then mumbles throughout the rest of the game, while everybody else is betting. He mumbles and hums tunes. It's pretty cute. His mind is always at work. If it's not at work on a tune, he's mumbling about a world event or something. He's very topical. When Johnny's not there, we don't laugh as hard. But there are things said at that table that can never be said in public. Nobody is safe."

♠ Excerpted from "The Man Who Retired," *Esquire*, June 2002

MEMBERS ONLY

by Starlee Kine

L AST YEAR I went to Las Vegas to cover the World Series of Poker for my job. I'm a documentary radio producer. I watched the best players in the world compete against each other. At the end of each day I drilled them for hours about their techniques and tactics. I made them play sample hands with me. Sometimes they let me win to boost my confidence and I'd yell at them, "But how will I ever learn!" and push my chair away from the table. I bought the definitive guide to Texas hold 'em. It was a heavy, leather-bound book with gold lettering on the cover, very sharp. When I flew home I didn't pack it in my suitcase, but carried it on the plane under my arm so the stewardesses and security guards would see and think me a hustler.

I came back to Chicago inspired. I fancied myself a real pro. The game of cards meant something to me. It was existential, just like the way Kenny Rogers said it was. I was eager to test out my chops. I talked to some friends and we decided to form a poker club. There were seven of us. We'd meet every Monday, these easy marks and myself, alternating apartments every week.

The boys rolled up their sleeves like Paul Newman and allowed a fine mist of young man's chin stubble to sprout. The girls wore long tight dresses and flowers in their hair. I found six green visors in a thrift store. The last person to show up had to wear a necktie around his head.

We came up with poker names. I was the Shark, because I had so much energy that I shook my knees until the table wobbled; if I stopped moving I'd die. Jay was Three Pairs because at first he thought three pairs could beat anything. He'd bet it all and then triumphantly, arrogantly even, turn over his cards, only to find out that he was sitting on a big fat pile of nothing. We shortened Cathay to Ay. Jason told us a story about this barbershop he used to go to in the suburbs. These old men had been going there every day for thirty years. One of them had only been going there for twenty years so they called him the new guy. We liked that, so Alison became New Girl. If her boyfriend came and played with us we called him New Girl too. Jason didn't have a nickname, but we could tell how badly he wanted one. He was always dropping hints.

We special-ordered poker chips. They had naked mermaids that swam along the edges. We spent hours trying to pick the perfect color combination. Finally we settled on lime green, black, and orange. The colors looked great together. We learned how to shuffle the chips together because of the clicking sound it made.

We bought snacks. Snacks that reminded us of movies and carpeting and video games and that made us feel cozy. Mallomars and cheese puffs and potato chips and ice cream with magic-shell topping. We filled every bowl in the house. We filled all the pots and pans, too. Pretzel rods were our favorite. I'd eat the salt off them like corn on the cob. Somehow we never got tired of making dumb sex jokes. Rod me, Kent, rod me. Cracked us up like a bunch of fifth-graders every time.

We bought beer. We made gin and tonics. We set a big bottle of whiskey in the center of the table. We got drunk and told everyone that we loved them.

We collected decks of cards. Catherine had inherited an art deco set from her grandmother. I found a deck with kittens on it for a dollar in the St. Louis airport. Our pride and joy, though, was the dirty deck a friend of mine had brought back from Greece. Illustrations of frisky Greeks doing it in every possible combination. Different numbers had different themes. Most themes were pretty straightforward. The threes were threesomes. Kings had masturbation, queens lesbianism. Others we never did quite figure out. The sixes theme involved a parakeet, a fox, a washboard, a candlestick, and at least four people, maybe five, although the fifth person could've been some sort of dancing imp. Sometimes you could tell who had the six just by the number of times they rotated it around, trying to get to the bottom of it once and for all.

We had everything we needed. Except none of us really knew how to play cards.

I tried to teach them everything I knew. I had them practice throwing their cards down in disgust. I showed them how to spread their chips into lots of different stacks so it looked like they had more money. I taught them that winners never chase.

I scrutinized everyone's poker face and then offered up suggestions. Cathay's was the best. She had a really great smirk. Whenever anyone else tried to do it, they just ended up looking obnoxious. My poker face consisted of me picking up a bottle of beer and reading the label over and over again hoping no one would notice that I'd suddenly gotten real quiet.

Whoever dealt got to choose the game we'd play. We had the gimmick games, like pass the trash and day baseball. We liked those the best. The real poker games never lasted all that long. We'd play a few hands of five-card draw and then everyone's interest would start to wane. We'd start talking about TV shows we liked. Inevitably someone would declare a wild card and I'd roll my eyes. Wild cards were for chumps. They don't have wild cards in Vegas. I'd stay moody until we switched games.

Texas hold 'em was the one real game we liked playing. It was the official game of the World Series. We loved saying "Here comes the

flop." But we never got any better at it. The way it goes is, you're
dealt two cards face down, and then five more cards are dealt face
up in the middle for everyone to share. You're supposed to fold if
your two cards aren't totally strong. But we never folded because we
all enjoyed playing too much. We all wanted to say "And down the
river comes fourth street." So we always lost all our money. No one
ever pulled ahead.

Since we never learned how to properly play, we'd get tired of all
the games fairly quickly. So we started trying to come up with new
games. There were a lot of duds. But then we came up with one that
actually stuck. It was called "screw the queen." It was very simple.
The highest card was the four of clubs and the lowest card was the
queen of hearts. If you got the queen of hearts you automatically
lost. And you couldn't trade it in until the end. There were three
rounds. The first round you got one card dealt to you face down that
you could look at. Then you bet. Second round you had the option
to trade in your card for a free one from the deck. Then you bet
again. In the third round you had the option to *buy* a new card for
a dollar, either from the deck or from one of your opponents. And
they had to give it to you, they had no choice. And they couldn't buy
it back. So if someone bought the four of clubs off you, you just had
to sit there and suck it up.

It was our greatest accomplishment. We couldn't stop high-fiving
each other across the table for having thought it up. It was everything that was fun about poker and nothing that was boring. And
since we'd made it up and were the only people who even knew the
rules, we were invincible. The best in the world. We could really get
into each other's heads. At one point Kent actually convinced Jay
that he could read his mind. Jay was never quite the same after that.

The poker club lasted six months. Little by little it fell apart. Kent
kept canceling because of band practice. We tried to make him
choose between us and the band but that didn't really work. Ay
started pastry-chef college. Three Pairs moved in with his girlfriend,

who didn't approve of us. New Girl moved to California with her boyfriend, New Girl. We tried to stay in touch. We went to the movies together a few times. That was awkward. That whole time we'd thought it hadn't really been about the cards, but once they were gone it was a lot harder to figure out what to talk about. Outside the game, it felt nerdy to use our poker names. We kept zipping our coats up and down and smiling nervously at each other, until it was time to go inside and watch the movie.

DID YOU EVER PLAY POKER?

CONVERSATIONS WITH ELDERLY CITIZENS AT MEAL SITES, SOCIAL CENTERS, AND NURSING HOMES

by David Greenberger

David Greenberger: Did you ever play poker?

Burdette Buckley: Yeah, I used to, just nickel-and-dime, small games. It was just little stuff down at the fire department. Al Foss, he used to play. There's only a couple of us left now.

◆

Bill Butz: I never played poker. Well, in the army we did. I remember some guys would get their pay and put the whole load of it right there on the table. They'd bet and lose it all.

Years ago we used to play euchre, that and, oh what was it . . . I haven't played in years. Boy oh boy, I can't remember. I don't think I'd know how to play it now anyway. It was a family game. I can't remember what it was called . . . oh! Pinochle was the one, that was the big one. Euchre and pinochle, pinochle was the biggest. Even my father from Germany played it, he said they liked it over there.

◆

Florence Perry: My grandchild tried to teach me to play poker, but I didn't do too well.

Helen Sheridan: Did it get expensive?

FP: It wasn't that, I just didn't understand it. I guess I'm not a good gambler.

◆

Jerry St. Clair: Poker? Hell, that's years ago, fella! They got into it at the veterans and the fire department meetings, there'd be games on Tuesday nights after the fire department meetings. But I haven't got into it anymore in the last years. I think the thing that got it stopped with the organizations was arguments they had between this, that, and the other one, so I got away from it. [Points to Helen, sitting beside him.] This one ought to play, she's lucky.

Helen St. Clair: I used to go over to the sawmill and take a cake over there and win all the money from the guys!

◆

Ed Veshecco: Strip poker! [laughs] Well, I didn't play really, I watched. I was just a kid. They was high school friends of my friend's sister. I was over there and they were havin' a party in the basement and drinkin' and everything. Of course, the parents weren't there. Then four or five of 'em starts playin' strip poker upstairs at the kitchen table. Two of the girls had their bras off, but I couldn't really see nothin'—it was kind of dark and they was sittin' low, you know, to try and hide themselves. Then the older brother came in and he didn't like what he saw goin' on. He yelled and the girls covered themselves up and the one guy who lost his pants hopped right out the door, pullin' 'em up out there in the snow. They made me go home too. I must've been about twelve or so.

◆

DG: Phebe, do you play cards?

Phebe Brown: Yes.

DG: What kind?

PB: What kind are there?

DG: Poker.

PB: No, I never played poker.

Helen Petteys: She doesn't gamble, don't you know that?

DG: Do you?

HP: No, I don't play cards.

DG [to Helen Sheridan]: Do you play poker?

Helen Sheridan: No, I don't play poker, I play pitch and 500.

HP: I can play old maid and go fish.

HS: Those are grade school games.

HP: Yes.

DG: But Phebe, you never played poker?

PB: No.

DG: I can't picture you tossing dice either.

PB: [laughs]

HP: She's very religious.

◆

Gene Weaver: I wished I could have been better educated. I wished I could have traveled more. I wished I could have climbed up the ladder a little further. But I'm not disappointed in what I did. I was a pattern maker, I worked in making things out of wood. When I say things, you wouldn't know what they were unless I told you. I've made some peculiar things in my line. I've had a lot of nuts who wanted to talk to me—that's no reflection on what you're doing [laughs]—but I've had a lot of nuts wanting to talk to me. [Still laughing.] Now maybe I shouldn't have said that. I'm sure you're a fine fellow and I'm sure you're not a nut, because if you were you wouldn't want to be talking to me like this, if you were a nut, I wouldn't guess anyway. Of course, one nut to another nut is all right, I guess. Well, you've got to have a little bit of humor.

People would come in and want me to make devices. I wasn't a device maker, I was a pattern maker. Of course, they didn't know the difference. This one guy, he wanted me to make him a device to strap on his arm that he could put playing cards in, that when he's playing cards that he could slip out what he wanted to. And I said, "You're just fixing to get your head blown off." I said, "Anybody who's playing cards where you're playing cards wouldn't mind shootin' you." I said, "The best thing you can do is forget about it because I'm not gonna make that for you."

I've had some crackpots, some real crackpots. I can't think of them all right now. Some of them come in and start talking to me and seem intelligent enough, they'll even have some drawings, but they turn out to be crackpots, with just plain crazy ideas.

remembrance of chips past

by Neal Pollack

T HE MEMORIES OF YOUTH pour across my mind like so much
sticky syrup when I get an assignment like the one for this
book. And since all first-person nonfiction these days seems to
involve unresolved inner conflicts with a relative, I'll make my con-
tribution to the genre. My particular bête noire is my grandfather.
But he was no prize-winning physicist or great scion of a New
England family. No. When I knew him, he was just a low-level manager for a small San Diego chemical-supply company, a frustrated
inventor, and generally a grumpy, bitter person, my personal Willy
Loman figure. The two-minute psychologist within says that
grandpa never lived up to the specter of his own father, who was the
chief justice of the Wisconsin State Supreme Court for a time in the
1930s, and a good friend of the fighting LaFollettes. Maybe I could
write a book on this topic, or at least do a piece for *This American
Life*. Ah, screw it. I'll just write this little piece and then get back to
doing what I'm really good at: promoting myself.

So while you keep the above background material in mind, my
recollection begins.

It was a summer afternoon, early 1980s, at my grandparents' little two-bedroom apartment in Pacific Beach, a low-rent building in
a high-rent neighborhood. I was at the dining-room table with my

grandfather and a couple of his buddies, surrounded by memorabilia celebrating the careers of Winston Churchill and Theodore Roosevelt, men my grandfather admired and in no way resembled. I was nine, or eight, or ten, or eleven. We were playing poker.

I'd been reading up on the game, and had played it with friends and cousins. Really, I wasn't too bad for my age. I understood the hierarchy of hands, and was decent at counting cards. But I'd never gambled before. And I was a wuss.

My grandpa dealt me some chips. I don't remember whether we were playing with real money or not, but he staked me regardless. Cards went around the table. I think it was five-card draw. My hand was pretty good. I anted. Grandpa grinned. His friends saw my opening bets, and then we discarded, and, well, you know how the game goes.

I bet wrong, in a way I don't remember, and got cleaned out. Grandpa dealt again. Again, I anted. The pattern repeated itself. These guys had been playing poker for fifty years. They were smacking me down.

The third hand was my downfall. I can't recall the specific hand, but I had good cards. The other guys at the table folded quickly. My grandpa didn't. He smirked me silly. I discarded, maybe one card, and still he stared. I bet. He raised. I raised his raise. He kept going up. His friends laughed. I got nervous. But I kept betting. He kept raising. Finally, he tossed in a bet, a really high one. I folded. He showed his cards. He had nothing.

His friends roared. He roared. I felt a raw tickle in my chest as I sunk in embarrassment. It was the first time I'd ever been truly had. They'd beaten me, and it wasn't just for that hand. The rest of the game was torment. Someone outdid me every time. They teamed up and I didn't win a single deal. But they kept laughing and mocking, and it wasn't friendly, either. They were devouring a weak member of the tribe, and there was no mercy. A little kid, too ashamed to weep, was out of chips, and they enjoyed themselves very much.

I never forgot the way my grandpa acted that day, and never really forgave him. But I have good memories, too. There was the time that his car broke down on the way back from an Arizona State game and he kept me amused in a foul-smelling sub shop next to a gas station, or the way he used to whistle college-football fight songs through the gaps in his false teeth, or how on Passover he used to tie up a napkin in the shape of a mouse and make it jump all around the table. He could be a really funny guy when he wasn't blind drunk on Canadian Club, or hissing at black people.

While certain other memories have stuck around, my twenty-year-old poker wound still bleeds my heart raw, and not because I lost. Lord knows I've lost enough subsequent games in my life since to recover from a superficial beating with no real stakes. The problem was, and still is, this: my grandfather, my elder, had a chance to teach me something, and instead he just submitted me to ritual shame. I contrast him with my dad, who sat through hundreds of boring games of backgammon with me until I got good enough to win without just getting lucky. If I screwed up, my dad told me how, and why. Grandpa never did that. Poker, an infinitely challenging game, offers many lessons for a young man. But for me they've gone unlearned to this day. I've never played poker again.

Just before he died, nearly ten years ago, I called my grandpa in the hospital. It was my birthday. His last words to me were, "You should go to Denny's. You'll get a free breakfast."

Such was the breadth of my grandfather's wisdom, and his infinitely enduring legacy.

THE PLAYERS

by Robert Elder

Willy

An intrepid traveler and self-styled frontiersman, Willy serves as the de facto leader of the weekly Riley College international poker game. The Wyoming-born card shark also brings the most obscene blasphemies and insults to the table, schooling our foreign friends on the intricacies of American cursing. He once said of his own girlfriend: "She's a carpenter's perfect woman—flat as a board and easy to nail." Our guardian of poker etiquette, he's often heard saying, "You'd get shot in Vegas for that."

Thomas

Most likely to be shot in Vegas. A bad winner and worse loser, Thomas gloats shamefully, even for an American. He hides food like a Turkish prisoner, refusing to share snacks or even insight into his own lame punch lines. On the upside, as soon as he loses his money, he leaves. He's clueless, although never in an endearing way. Whoever said, "If a man who cannot count finds a four-leaf clover, is he lucky?" must have known Thomas.

Constantine

A Russian poker enthusiast who—when beaten—exclaims "You cocksicker!"

"No," we say. "Cock*sucker*."

"What for do you discriminate against us Russians?" he asks, even though he's the only Russian national at the table, and the only player with an impotent pair of fours.

There's a failed attempt to explain the words "stomach pump" to him, its applications, and how it might come into play should he continue his rate of alcohol consumption.

"No," he insists, he could still ride his bicycle home with a stomach pump—and even a catheter—attached, if need be. "Weak Americans," he says.

Hyato

Perhaps the Japanese reincarnation of Wild Bill Hickok, Hyato loves Black Sabbath's "Iron Man" and, strangely, Heart's "Barracuda." Long, raven-black hair spilling out from under a baseball cap has become his poker uniform, his trademark—a handlebar mustache for the twenty-first century. Our resident headbanger remains loyal to wild-card Texas hold 'em and baseball poker (threes and nines wild, a four earning an extra card), which produce ridiculously gargantuan pots. He's most dangerous when he goes silent. Legend tells that Hickok was shot in the back of the head while playing poker, the bullet exiting his right cheek, two pair in his hand: aces and eights. No one dares draw on Hyato, even when he's holding a "dead man's hand" with his back to the door.

Shannon

The only one of us to understand the nuances of numeric destiny and the sharp edge of luck, brave Shannon remains the lone woman of the group. She will win the Big Game at the end of the year, a nearly $100 pot. Other players alternately rush to defend her honor and take her money. By the end of her first year with us, Shannon knows more about the life, times, and measurements of improbably endowed porn star John Holmes than she cares to.

Lenny

Born in Thailand, Lenny considers himself Japanese. Or Chinese. No one can really keep it straight, but he's entertainingly neurotic and the guy most likely to go the distance on any hand, regardless of his cards. His games are seven-card stud and five-card draw, often with twos wild.

Nearly six feet tall, Lenny is also deathly afraid of chickens. No one is really sure why. Once, we joked about putting a chicken in his room. "Don't make me kill you," he said, seriously still. "I don't want to kill you." Shannon later finds out that Lenny has a recurring night terror in which he's caught in the middle of a poultry-filled room. That's it, the whole nightmare. "Peep," the chickens taunt him. "Peep."

Yogi

The only person known to get six of a kind in a five-card game and go unchallenged, this round Indonesian slings a dangerous smile and an infectious laugh. Yogi is also a cheatin' bastard. We let him play anyway, as no one has the heart to excommunicate him. Besides, no one else knows how to deal from the bottom of the deck, and we all want to learn.

Regardless, his bluffs are like black holes. Everyone falls in.

Steve

Responsible for more ruined decks of cards than any other player, by way of spilled beer. Swaying, with bloodshot eyes, Steve will inevitably knock over his Heineken during the fourth hour of play.

He keeps his coins in a grenade-shaped jar.

More than once, Steve has disappeared to fuck one of the redheads on the third floor, only to return to the table afterward with appallingly boring sex stories. "I just went in there, did my business, and left."

"Did she cum?" Willy says, concerned.

"I don't know."

"Did you at least cuddle with her?"

"I just went in there and did my business."

"What?! There's a mandatory amount of cuddle time after each coupling," Willy says, disgusted. "You're making us look bad."

Spencer

A small-town American boy, Spencer speaks German and Spanish, and looks uncannily like a young Jack Kerouac. High Chicago is his game, in which the player with the highest spade in the hole reaps half the pot. It's a smart defensive choice, a game easily played when drunk.

During his sophomore college year, Spencer and Steve will become roommates in a putrid petri dish of an apartment, where they both will brew beer. A mummified cat Steve found while cleaning barns will be kept under the couch in a shoebox, carted out to impress and horrify company. The kitty will be sent to Willy, who will have moved back to Wyoming. The "Patriarch of the Prairie" will in turn use it to torture his neighbors as a "watch cat" perched on his porch. A few days later, the petrified feline will be found inside his screen door, with a policeman's business card hooked in its perma-snarling mouth.

Hogan

After watching *King Kong*, Hogan knew he wanted to study primates. He gets a head start by observing us. "Monkeys and great apes thrive not on instinct alone, but on the weight of experience and their degree of need," Hogan says. "They aren't dumb animals, but noble brokers of chance, sensitive to malleable rules of adaptation . . . "

"Shut up and deal," we interrupt.

Besides, we prefer Mario Puzo's take: " . . . man's instinct to gamble is the only reason he is still not a monkey up in the trees."

Rob

The craft of poker requires some flair for metaphor, some hyperbolic sense of drama. An aspiring writer, Rob wants to understand this. After all, writing is the craft of manipulation, of lying to tell bigger truths. How good a poker player this makes him has yet to be seen. A borderline insomniac, Rob loves the velocity of play, the lexicon of cards, the camaraderie of chance. Odds are, he'll spend the remainder of his life trying to recreate his college poker experience. He'll fail miserably, and write about it instead.

POKER FOR PENNIES

by Nikki Stewart and Jacqueline Stewart

Yᴏᴜ'ʀᴇ ɴᴇᴠᴇʀ ᴛᴏᴏ ʏᴏᴜɴɢ to start playing poker. At least that's what our Nana thought, so every Saturday when we were over at her house we would play poker for pennies. One of us girls had to go down in the basement and grab the fishbowl full of pennies that Nana and Auntie kept under the bar. Once back upstairs, we would divide the coins into even-looking piles and begin to play. We learned all the standard games like five-card draw and five- or seven-card stud, but our favorites were the ones where a whole bunch of cards were wild—games like "low hole and center" and "eights and after aces." Sometimes we'd make two or three different cards wild even in draw or stud.

Even though we played with real money, it never seemed like you could lose. We always felt, as little people, like there was hope and magic working in our favor. That's why we had so many wild cards. We didn't play to beat one another—we played to enjoy the magic of seeing the next card dealt after that ace in eights and after aces. It could look like you were losing all the way up to that point, but once an ace appeared your whole situation could change in an instant. Silly little low cards that have been sitting in your hand with absolutely no promise would suddenly get up and dance, because their red or black sister got dealt after that ace! And if things got too bad and you started to run out of pennies, Nana would always slide some of hers over to you so you could keep playing.

At Nana's house the adults would play poker, too. The grown-up poker games would break out every time there was a large family gathering at Nana's house. On weekends and holidays, or when word got out that Nana had made one of her big wonderful meals, relatives from all over Chicago would make their way down to the basement of Nana's and Auntie's house, where there was a special card table lined with green felt and decorated with hearts, spades, clubs, and diamonds. Although the kids were never allowed to play in the adult games (we weren't supposed to stay in the basement too long) we could hang around sometimes as cocktail waitresses delivering their drinks.

We found out from Nana that when our mother and her cousins were kids in the late 1940s and early 1950s, they would hang around the poker table as well. Back in those days, these were not only friendly family games, but also regular Friday night events including acquaintances—mostly men our grandfather knew—to raise money. Nana's job at these games was to "cut the pot"—take a certain percentage of the ante and each round of bets off the top as a profit.

Just like in Las Vegas, drinks were served freely at these games, and "the house" profited more and more as the players loosened up. When we asked our mother about this, she told us that she and the other kids in the family loved these games as a source of income as well. In addition to collecting "tips" from the players for delivering their drinks, as the evening progressed the kids would crawl under the poker table to retrieve and keep money that the players inevitably dropped on the floor as their intoxication increased and their concentration decreased.

Those kids who played under the table during our mother's generation became the grown-ups playing in the family games we remember. Our mother, aunts, uncles, cousins, and even Nana would get in on the action. Although they started off playing draw and stud, over the years they started playing our wild card games too, enjoying the wonder and surprise that we did. The grown-ups played for real money, and would occasionally get angry when they lost, but the games were always about enjoying each other's company. They laughed and sang more than they fought. Records were always spinning on the turntable, and when Bobby "Blue" Bland sang, "You'll be a millionaire," everyone believed it might come true that night. There was also B. B. King, the Spinners, Gladys Knight and the Pips, and, our favorite, the O'Jays. We found out later that even when the grown-ups played "serious" games of poker, if one of them ran out of money someone else would slip them some so they could stay in the game.

As we girls have become women we haven't really kept up with our poker. It's harder to get the family together these days, and at our last poker party we were all so happy to see each other we never got around to breaking out the cards. That wouldn't have happened if Nana was around. She lived to be eighty-six. Until the end of her days on earth, she enjoyed playing cards for fun and for money. I guess you're never too old to play poker either.

CHASE THE ACE,
OR POKER AS CLASS WARFARE

by Jeremy Braddock

I DON'T KNOW BOO ABOUT POKER (which is part of the point of this story), so it is probably appropriate that I keep this short. Nineteen ninety-five was the first summer I spent in New York, and it was a hot one. My roommate John and I had an apartment on the Lower East Side that enjoyed a roof from which you could see a lot. My abiding memory of that summer is sitting on the roof and looking at the mauve crown of smog that, until September, gathered over Manhattan before moving down south to finish off those ice caps.

Anyway, I had moved to New York to start grad school at NYU. I had lived the past three years in San Francisco, and my girlfriend Chris had also left SF, to go to grad school in Virginia. That summer, she was sweating it out with John and me in our apartment by night, as we all temped during the day. Chris worked for a while for the then-nascent TV Food Network while I put in a few weeks clock-watching at a public-relations firm whose clients included Shaquille O'Neal (rap album division) and Christie Brinkley (damage control for divorce from Billy Joel division).

The summer of temping rightly identified us as belonging to that subsection of the college-educated middle class that had neither the connections nor their shit sufficiently together to be making more money. Despite splitting the rent three ways, we were feeling very fucking broke. Which made it both a relief and also kind of galling to know that our better-heeled friends from California, Daisy and JP, were also in New York that summer, living large and looking to play some poker.

In hindsight, I can see with more clarity the particular sociology of this friendship. Chris and I were at this point every bit as over-educated as they were, and were even about to surpass them. But there was a narcissism of class difference that nevertheless felt very acute. As I maybe incorrectly remember, Daisy was the daughter of a wealthy California lumberman. I didn't know about the provenance of JP. In either event, the critical point was that this summer they were living in the kind of New York apartment that we always knew was "there," but never figured on experiencing firsthand. It was on the seventeenth floor of a Gothic apartment building a few blocks west of Columbus Circle, and was directly adjacent to the building that had been the exterior location for the bourgeois lesbian-panic freak-out film *Single White Female*. It had not one, but two balconies, and though it was small it occupied several slightly different levels. Needless to say, it was air-conditioned. To me, it looked like a fantastic place to get laid for twelve hours a day, and read and write for the other twelve.

This apartment was a good symbol for our friendship with Daisy and JP. We genuinely liked them, but we had the faint suspicion that their ease with the world (ease at getting better paying jobs than we could get, ease with crypto-slumming [did I mention their motorcycles], ease with hanging with us as well as their class equals) communicated something about a significant slice of privilege that we'd never enjoyed.

These details, as well as the density of the heat, which seemed to get more pronounced *after* the sun went down, had me feeling especially cranky. We took the 1/9 train north to Columbus Circle, and

I picked a fight with Chris as a way of entertaining myself. We bought a six of Brooklyn Lager at a bodega on the corner and turned left off Broadway to their building, recovering slightly from our bad mood at the novel sight of a uniformed doorman. We were welcomed into the apartment and shown to the south balcony. As we sat down and opened a beer, I realized that through some Freudian act, I had not thought to bring any money, much less change. Daisy and JP insisted that I shouldn't worry, they had a big jar of change and who cares anyway. I couldn't think of this gesture in any terms other than patronization. I leapt to the elevator and ran back down the street to get what was close to my last $20 from my account. Fuck it, even though I didn't expect to walk out of that apartment with any of my cash, I wasn't going to be a sucker.

When I returned we sat down and began to chill out, with our beer and a deck of cards. I should note that my knowledge of poker (I think I may speak for Chris, too) extended to five-card draw and an old chestnut we called "Indian," in which each player puts a single card face-up on his forehead and places bets based on his knowledge of everyone's cards but his own. Also I think I'd played a couple of stud games and one mysteriously titled "blind baseball." I'm pretty sure the last time I'd played poker it had been for nickel candy.

I offered that I knew of blind baseball, but could he remind me how it was played. With a slight air of disgust, JP took to instructing us in the games he wished to play, dealing the cards, and then playing the hand. One particularly memorable game was euphoniously titled "chase the ace, bury the bitch." We were still feeling like we were looking in the window of Barney's, but we were certainly enjoying drinking beer at such an elite (and comfortably air-conditioned) location.

One more digression: To beat the heat, Chris and I spent a great deal of this summer playing pinball (our favorite tables being "Theater of Magic" and "Twilight Zone"). Although I still take it seriously, the beauty of pinball is that, even though it masquerades as a game of skill, talent is not required to have a good game. Chris, whose technique consisted of *always* simultaneously hitting both flippers, won half the games we played. I had always assumed that poker was closer to the pool side of the skill/knowledge continuum, which is one reason I've always been slightly suspicious of the game. But this golden evening produced evidence of an unexpected kind.

Which is to say *we fucking kicked their ass at every goddamn hand of poker all night long!* And I, with my humble twenty, especially shone in this crepuscular contest. Over the next several hours good cards kept coming our way. Consequently, the increasing exasperation on JP's face made our task all the easier (not to mention more enjoyable). His non-poker face allowed us to get bolder in our betting and bluffing. With my lonely twenty of recommendation, I walked home with pockets only slightly heavier than Chris's. Though the specifics of the evening wane in my memory, these images stick with me: the repeated sequences of being quickly instructed in the principles of a new game, the dealing of the cards, a round of betting, significant assessments of the participants' facial affects, another round of betting, our eventual victory, and finally the increasing stages of JP's exasperation (though he managed to remain, on the whole, amenable to our presence).

We didn't hook up with Daisy and JP again that year, though I wouldn't necessarily chalk that up to our exhibition of innate skill at the art of poker. But that evening did endow Chris and me with a good vibe that lasted for the remainder of the summer. And needless to say, it sponsored many future pursuits of that exalted expression of democratic pluralism known by the name of . . . pinball!

no one gets Hurt

by Chris Tsakis

I'VE BEEN AROUND a poker table since I could walk upright under one. My mother's side of the family played whenever two or more of them gathered. The games occurred mostly at my grandmother's. My brothers and I were usually the only males around. We existed largely unseen in a world of women, all very vocal and loud. They'd chew the fat for a bit, then the cards and the chips would come out and someone would make manhattans or martinis. The ritual would begin.

There were always plenty of alcoholic beverages, and a cloud of cigarette smoke hung over the table. My mother liked Kools. My Aunt Georgie smoked Camels. My Aunt Iz was all about Pall Malls. She might've been my favorite and she wasn't even blood. She was from Ocala, Florida, but came up north toward the end of World War II to work at Grumman building planes. Her fiancé was a flyer and died over Europe. She moved in upstairs with my grandparents.

On summer nights in the enclosed porch—lightning bugs flashing outside, poker chips clicking, everyone laughing—Aunt Iz would say, "Chris, go to the Frigidaire and get me a beer, would you?" I'd fetch one from the ever-present six-pack of Ballantine Ale parked way in the back, behind the ginger ale and vegetables. I'd open it with a church key, take a sip unseen before handing it over. A stream of gossip would wind its way around and through the fabric of the game. I'd try to concentrate while they shuffled, dealt, and bet over and over. They'd play for hours. When I got too underfoot, my grand-mother would hand me the garage key and tell me to go "play."

My father shipped home a 1949 Mercedes from Germany before he was discharged from the army. The Benz ended up in my grand-mother's garage. When I'd worn out my welcome at the poker games, I'd run like hell the fifty feet to the garage—never avoiding the mos-quitoes swarming—unlock the door, click on the light, open the sui-cide door, and climb into deep tan leather. I'd grab the wheel and go BRUMMM-BRUMMM-BRUMMM until I usually fell asleep.

Years later, when I was old enough to sip beer out in the open, I moved to New Jersey. I was living in Tenafly, and on my first night there my friend Jeff drove me down to Tom's and Jim's basement apartment on Hudson Street in Hoboken. They were having some kind of get-together, I don't think it was a party. A bunch of people sat around on chairs, drinking beer, bullshitting. Later we played poker, a makeshift game with matchsticks for chips.

When Tom brought out the matchsticks and the cards, I was gen-uinely excited (I hadn't played poker in years—and never with peo-ple besides my relatives). Five of us sat around the kitchen table, and when the smoke cleared hours later, I had done pretty well for myself. I think I cleared six or seven dollars.

The same crew would get together every few weeks and play, always a nickel ante (our motto: "No One Gets Hurt—A Friendly Game"). As the game grew older the equipment got upgraded, first to antique celluloid chips, then plastic after I found a chip tray and chips at a flea market. Tom bought a special poker table that folded up and went behind his couch. We used Bicycle cards, a standard deck. We drank lots of cheap beer and blasted the Ramones. It became a weekly thing. The game grew, sometimes to nine people (being a bit of a poker purist, I'd argue for splitting the game at that point). I printed up a business-card-sized Pocket Poker Peeker, to ease confusion about the rank of hands. The game ran smoothly for years, and I won a decent share of pots. Then it began a slide into hellishness.

Women had ushered me into the poker world decades earlier, and they would, ultimately (through no fault of their own), show me the exit. Nancy, Thaler, and Betty constituted the Ladies Auxiliary, and I made the mistake of hitting on one too many of the ladies. First Nancy. We went out once, but I subsequently came on too strong and made an ass of myself. I moved on to Thaler. She politely rebutted my pass and continued to come to the game. Eventually, I asked her if Betty was "available." Probably not my best idea. Things got chilly after that, especially when it became apparent that Tom had eyes for Thaler. I had transgressed once too often and was soon frozen out of a pretty good poker game. I eventually got Tom on the phone and asked why no one told me about the games anymore. He explained, "You've worn out your welcome."

And me with no garage or Mercedes Benz to run to.

BEATING PAUL

by Tom Spurgeon

WE PLAYED POKER in the mid-1990s because we had nothing better to do. My friends and I, all of the age when moving out of your parents' home a second time became a good idea, worked in one of the few branches of the Pacific Northwest economy that failed to make its bright and eager youth into wealthy-on-paper adults. While everyone around us made either real fortunes or the equivalent in life experiences, we toiled as office functionaries and grunt-level copy editors for an alternative comic-book company. They were the kind of jobs that became "I work in publishing," if you wished to avoid instant pity from the person who asked. We were too broke to buy our own fun, and the vast majority of us were too socially inept to make it from scratch. Playing poker with the gang from work allowed for a cheap night out and an opportunity to talk to members of the opposite sex who didn't frighten us or frighten easily. It was almost like doing something fun.

For months our games were amiable, diverting, and frighteningly dull. Players wandered off to the restroom and never returned. Others showed up late to halfheartedly deny to a jury of their peers, more jealous than disdainful, that they had been catching a favorite television show. A few regulars never bothered learning the basic rules of the game, and had to be reminded from game to game how to bet and which hands beat which other hands. They sat there with beatific Harpo Marx smiles and piles of change they would refuse to convert into chips, annoying everyone. If poker games, like empires, have a natural life span, then by its sixth month ours was ready to have sex with its relatives and elect a horse to the Senate.

Then our employers hired Paul. Arriving in early 1996, he was everything Seattle's relentless mellowness (and an hourly wage suited to summer camp counselors) had beaten out of the rest of us. Paul was enthusiastic, confrontational, and bouncily aggressive. And he was loud. Teenagers-on-a-bus loud. Sylvester Stallone–yelling-out-the-window loud. In the mornings you could hear Paul stomping through the outer rooms of the office like the aural equivalent of the kiddie footprints in "Family Circus," his bellowed shouts of "Good Morning!" marking his location through walls and punishing any-one who stood in his way. We liked him, feared him, and wondered out loud how long he could possibly remain employed at a firm that trumpeted its laid-back working environment the way other com-panies touted their dental plans.

Yet for all the reasons Paul didn't quite fit in at work, he saved our lives at the poker table. Paul played every hand of poker like an actor tossing aside his cape for his final encore. The force of his per-sonality shook the lethargy from us like so many spoiled children. With high-decibel cries of "Gotta be in it to win it!" and "You snooze, you lose!" and hands that lunged across the table after win-nings like a drunkard eager to arm wrestle, Paul gave our game a much-needed focus. Everyone soon had the same two goals.

1. Play like Paul.
2. Beat Paul.

It wasn't going to be easy. But after a third week of ending our Thursdays listening to Paul count his money at the table, in direct violation of a Kenny Rogers core value, we dug in.

Three weeks after Paul joined the game, people stopped arriving late. Players who couldn't remember the rules were given a sheet of winning hands and warned to shut up in the manner of adults accosting teenagers at the beginning of a family outing. The game soon swelled to include more players than one table and one deck of cards could safely handle. The table that lacked Paul furiously craned its necks as shouts of anger and gleeful payback emanated from across the room, sending individuals over every half hour to see if seating assignments could be revised. Thursday nights had become Thursday Nights, something to be discussed, anticipated, and strategized over. Paul's aggressive betting raised nickel-ante stakes to a potential evening's-end windfall of $30 or $40, just enough to break double digits, percentage-wise, in comparison to our weekly paychecks. Couples met, dated, broke up, and no one cared because we were all too busy trying to beat Paul. Ex-employees, who normally avoided the old gang in time-honored Prince Hal fashion, began to put aside real social opportunities for a chance to continue after a piece of Paul.

It ended with an extended wheeze. As the wet and cold part of spring became only the wet part, Paul gave notice—disturbing his coworkers immensely by remaining quiet for a full day—and began to look for opportunities out of state. An interim job taken in the summer heat made him an irregular presence at the poker table, sometimes not playing at all and other times playing just a few hands a session, during which the tension levels shot straight to the moon. Attendance dipped, and as the summer stretched into July, all that remained were the core four or five players that had made up the initial group. Paul played one last full session a couple of weeks before his departure to graduate school, shamelessly and happily browbeating us as he took multiple hands of seven-twenty-seven. We rose to the challenge—beer runs became beer-and-bank runs as food budgets were quickly revised in each of our heads. But by one o'clock we were spent, soaked with sweat, giddy at a game that had left not a single person down more than $2. "I wish I could say it's been fun—but it hasn't," Paul said, for once at a reasonable volume. Everyone smiled.

Paul barreled out of town a few weeks later, and the poker game must have been in the trunk of his muscle car, because it sure didn't stick around Seattle for very long. We played intermittently for the next few years. It always seemed like a good idea. Some of those games would become ugly scenes where someone's guest would be, upon making eye contact with the original game's veterans, dubbed "The New Paul" and ganged up on mercilessly. More often, the sessions would dissolve into stories—about how Paul would routinely slap the table in victory, or, when losing, mutter a disconcerting non sequitur, perhaps about graphic sexual favors received in Las Vegas, that would throw some players completely off their game. He remained our friend, but we missed him as an enemy. Poker needs its Pauls.

GHE FLIGHT GAME

by Brett Forrest

I T WAS A three-hour layover in Denver, so I got buried in a bar
across from my gate. I was into a few of those proud Colorado
beers when a crew of guys stormed the table next to mine. They were
all mismatched. A couple of them were huge, covered in scruff and
briars. One was a hipster kid in big mirrored shades. Another rolled
up in a chalk-striped suit and a Don Rumsfeld haircut. This last one
slid a deck of cards from his leather briefcase and dealt a hand of
seven-card stud.

It looked like a dollar ante. I craned my neck to see. One of the
mean-looking guys had a tangled rug of chest hair pluming out of
his shirt like a backcountry ascot. He caught me looking and I froze.
"You play poker?" he snorted.

So I pulled up a chair. Next hand was hold 'em. This wasn't a
home game, but it felt like one. Nature scenes covered the walls. A
hockey game played low on the TV in the corner. The guys at the
table were cozy enough to scratch and burp. They grunted more than
they spoke. When they did speak, it was generally to raise.

I didn't say much either, believing that the new guy's betting
should handle the introductions. But I did meditate on it all, these
misfits playing for money out in the open at the airport Mile High
Saloon. There were no chips, just singles and fives and a few coins,

and as each pot grew, I wondered how long it would be before the bar shut us down.

A clutch of drafts in her hands, a waitress arrived at the table. Her eyes darted toward the pile in the middle of the table, but she didn't say anything. I figured it looked like a tip. Then something happened that I didn't register for many hours, until I was in the clouds up over Missouri somewhere. The waitress laid down the beers, and with a trace measure of ridicule, she said, "Nice cards, Glen."

a poker Family tree

by Ruth Lopez

I STARTED SITTING IN on a game in Santa Fe in 1995, where the core group had been playing together for more than twenty years. They were the descendants of a poker club that had been meeting since the fifties. Santa Fe has always been a haven for the wayward, the tubercular, heirs, heiresses, queers, artists, or any combination thereof. For the most part, these were the constituents of poker night, a historical amalgam of wealthy black sheep and their Boy Fridays. The few early female players were dames—one, the scion of a timber industry giant, arrived wearing white evening gloves and kept them on the entire game.

There was an air of formality to our low-stakes evening, albeit western-style. As far as distinctions go it's a slim one; this was not a poker party, rather an evening of cards with food and drink. The games were regular and started promptly. A copy of *Hoyle's* was always nearby to settle the rare dispute. We never put in more than ten bucks in the kitty to start.

The game rotated between several houses, but there was always the same poker carousel—an authoritative and gorgeous piece made of three different types of wood with inlay. It had belonged to one of the original players, Tommy Milne, a nephew of *Winnie-the-Pooh* author A. A. When Tommy died in the early 1970s, the carousel that had belonged to his father stayed with the club.

Over the years there were new arrivals to the game, arguably less colorful, and certainly poorer. Long gone was the dapper player with the hundred-dollar bill, hidden in his pocket watch, that he used to replenish his stock of chips. The dining aspect of the evening devolved from served steaks to potluck. The game, however, continued regularly and on time.

Like any self-respecting place in the West, New Mexico has its share of gambling legends and poker-playing outlaws. Billy the Kid played poker through the Lincoln County jailhouse cell bars with the deputy. In Santa Fe there was Maria Gertrudis Barcelo, known as Doña Tules, who opened a casino in the late 1820s. She bailed out the local government several times with her profits. Home poker may have been illegal, but it was hard to take any law seriously in light of such history and in a town where there was still an ordinance on the books outlawing fandangos.

As with any group that spends time together, we developed our own customs, language, and variations on games. When someone ran out of money in "chasey acey," a holdover of a game from Tommy's navy days, we hummed a dirge. Tom favored one-eyed jacks as wild cards. We created a game of blind guts called "I married Satan" that would exasperate any serious player. It was only called on evenings when there seemed to be a collective need to be utterly silly.

Everyone had their game. David liked to call for "Omaha lame-brain pea," because he loved the concept of shared cards. It was, he often said, his socialist game. You could count on Toby, a sort of free-market soul, to call for "shopping" because he liked the idea of buying a better hand. I leaned toward "Cincinnati crisscross," a nod perhaps to my preference for a mixed economy.

Rosie brought "Westchester" from New York, and the gang created a chase-the-queen variation dubbed "Winchester." It was banned for a few months after one night when the game, which probably went more than two dozen hands, just wouldn't end.

There were the nights following the opera when each dealer trilled the call with a faux falsetto and we would behave like a pack of demented divas—behavior any outsider might find insupportable. Eventually, in an effort to get back to the basics, someone would call for a sobering game of five-card draw. If a dealer was feeling particularly puritanical, the call would be for five-card stud.

Occasionally a visiting parent would sit in on a game and bring another generation's favorite to attention. KK's mother, who was in her late seventies, taught us "up and down the river." Playing poker with the gang was a highlight of her visit to town, and she generally managed to clean us out. Someone's grandparent introduced a dice game that produced the most expensive pots ever.

Rad, who had the most stable living conditions of the group over the years, was the caretaker of the carousel. He often hosted a game, and one of his house rules was to never seat more than seven people at the table. An evening of gaming at his home was always more focused, but no less fun, so it was hard for me to imagine I could ever commit a faux pas. But I did.

One evening, when the banter did not interest me as much as a cover story in a news magazine on a nearby counter, I reached over and picked it up and got completely absorbed in the read. I continued playing, I continued reading, and I was winning. It was a comfortable scenario for me, kind of like being at home as a child, where I was allowed to read at the dinner table and managed to never miss any important family news. This mental split-screen ability probably served me well years later, when I had to write in a noisy newsroom.

But the next week, I didn't get the call to play. And the following week I called to find out the when-and-where and learned that there were seven players already lined up. I had been demoted to the B-list of backup players, and I barely made it back into the club's good graces before moving away.

On a recent trip to New Mexico I learned that another newcomer had been disinvited for playing too aggressively, which made me look like a saintly crusader for literacy. When I ran into Rad at a party on that visit, he told me to let him know in advance next time I was coming to town so he could plan a poker night for me. I couldn't have heard anything sweeter. My first poker family was welcoming me home.

BOBBY BARE ON POKER

An Interview by Ken Burke

Bobby Bare is one of country music's most innovative, versatile legends. His forty-year-plus career has yielded such hits as "Detroit City," "500 Miles Away from Home," "Miller's Cave," and "Dropkick Me Jesus (Through the Goalposts of Life)." Here he talks to Ken Burke about country-music poker games.

Bobby Bare: We used to have a regular poker game years ago back in the '60s, where all the music people got together and played once a week.

Ken Burke: Who was involved in that?

BB: Doyle Wilburn, Grady Martin, Porter Wagoner, Ernest Tubb before he died—different ones.

KB: What were the stakes like?

BB: Well, it could get real hairy. It'd get real strong when everybody had money.

KB: Do you have any favorite memories of those poker games?

BB: Well, just the fact that when Ernest Tubb played he'd never fold. He'd stay in—I guess he was an optimist. We used to have jillions of poker games on the road. I remember we finished a show in San Antone—I believe it was me, George Jones, and Roy Clark. We had Monday off, so we played poker all night Sunday and all day Monday.

KB: How could you play that long without getting tired?

BB: Well, back then everybody was taking pills.

KB: [Laughs.] Should I quote you?

BB: Well, it was true.

WHEN IT CAME TO POKER, I DIDN'T GIVE A SHIT

by Jillian Steinberger

WHEN I THINK OF POKER, I don't think about the tangible aspects of the game, like the rules. I never learned them.

Nor do I think of Las Vegas. Gambling is not what comes to mind. I don't think of Chicago mafiosos hunched around a table, elbow to elbow in a dank cellar, acrid, billowing smoke from their fat cigars drifting up toward one swinging bulb; nor of dusty frontier towns in Ye Olde West, where mustachioed men once tipped back in their chairs and spied each other over their hands, vulnerable with their Stetsons politely removed for the hooch-hustling saloon ladies who'd lavish their attentions on the winner of the pot. The media—the *Godfathers* and *Bonanzas*—did not inculcate the economy of desire in me à la poker. I didn't give a shit, not in the least.

However, a time did come when I had cause to care, when poker became meaningful, and a range of associations attached themselves to that five-letter word. Now it evokes memory, time, and place. If you say it now, I think of words like: porch party, kitchen table, Marlboro Reds, sore throat, punk rock, cheap beer, cheap-beer runs, cicadas, verdant summertime, overgrown flowers, white picket fence, snowy winter, crunching snow, 3:00 A.M., belly laughs, waterheads, retards, vintage dresses, dogs and babies, red lipstick, Doc Martens, youth, Mary Jane, the state of being a girlfriend-appendage, "chesting," and something on the order of dyslexia.

There are stories within stories, and my story is that there's been one time in my life and one time only when I played poker. This was a regular Saturday night gig among bohemian rocker friends. I was the girlfriend who could never really figure out how to play, among cutthroat nickel-ante players. Maybe it was a learning disability. My impulses were just wrong; I felt affection for my friends—perhaps that's why I didn't care if I lost the pot to them. A refugee with less than zero from Beverly Hills via New York and Kathmandu, I sought safety and sanity under the benevolent wing of Mother Wisconsin and the easygoing company of Midwesterners. That was my win.

A commonly asked question was, "Why would you move from L.A. to Madison?!" But I wasn't a complete anomaly. Together we formed a young(ish) "couples set," fascinated by odd Jell-O-mold configurations at the Elks Club a couple blocks away.

We lived within walking distance to Madison's near east side, a neighborhood of massage therapists, pagans, vegans, students, politicos, punks, young families, and the Museum of Temporary Art. Familiar faces came and went, but a few formed the core contenders for stiff and drunken games: Dan and Anita, Sue and Eric, and my sweetheart, Mark, and myself. Sometimes Nancy and Al, visual artists, came; and Nancy's brother Chip and his girlfriend Gita. And though I never really learned how to play the game—not for lack of trying—I did learn a lot about the players. The unusual observations I drew have remained with me over the years.

Games took place around the cast-off wooden industrial spool that formed the coffee table at Sue's and Eric's lived-in flat on Spaight Street. We'd be full of glee and mischief, like little kids playing Stratego. Yet these were equal opportunity games and the antes were always a nickel, although highly sought-after quarters flew to the center of the table fast, a healthy $40 to $50 by quitting time.

We were obviously in it for the game more than the money, which simply fueled a sense of impish competition. So, while a couple of smug, lucky winners would go home with pockets full of change and an attitude, all of us would leave refreshed—if drunk—from one more work-week evening full of laughs and comradery among friends.

Playing styles varied. Anita was a rock, cupping her cards tightly, betting conservatively, and folding early. Her posture was erect, her face inexpressive, and she spoke in a calculated manner. She rarely lost, but she also rarely gained. In contrast, Mark was a wild, gesticulating maniac who got a kick out of roguishly fucking with his friends' heads and spicing up the games. Seven-card stud was our base game, but Mark would call fancier plays, changing games with each hand. Sometimes the lowest hand would win. Sometimes the best hand, the 7-5-4-3-2s, the straights, the flushes, or the full houses would count against you. We often played with a fifty-three-card deck because we liked the joker—he was wild, and wild cards let us be creative with the rules. But overall, these were pretty friendly games marked by slow plays. The stronger players would sometimes play their hands weakly so the weaker players could stay in the pot. And they'd coach.

Huber Bock, at under $5 a case, was Wisconsin's beer for everyman, rich, dark, and cheap. After our first case was gone, there'd be a beer-and-cigarette run to the tax-shelter town of Maple Bluff, which housed the governor's mansion (where I worked as a gardener the summer before graduate school until I hosed down the plush velour interior of the chief cook's car), and where spirits were sold until 2:30 A.M. Hoarse and smelly from chain smoking—the ashtray would have been dumped countless times—and shouting above the racket of music and voices, at 3:00 or 4:00 A.M. Mark and I would tramp home in the crunchy snow, or stroll arm in arm in the summer warmth, to our four cats curled up in the basement-in-a-chateau we called home on Rutledge Street, right on the lake, across from the park.

Dan and Anita hosted games too, in their roomy, futuristic 1950s pad, a couple blocks over from Eric and Sue. A little stardust blew off Dan, the sludgy drummer of an underground band known as Killdozer, which had an insane sense of humor and not a little substance—their first album, for instance, was titled *Intellectuals are the Shoeshine Boys of the Ruling Elite*. One of the first bands on the independent Touch and Go label, Killdozer was produced by the master of analog recording himself, Steve Albini, and by Garbage's Butch Vig, who also produced *Nevermind* for Nirvana.

Over a hand at the kitchen table one frosty December evening, Dan had us sick with belly laughter over wicked yet sympathetic stories of his day job as orderly at a home for the differently abled. The retarded men and women often tried to fuck. He, himself, had found a couple fucking between mealtimes in the dining room. He had had to call for help to pull the copulators apart. He felt sad about it: no sex for retards—was it fair? Gazing at our navels, we pondered.

Dan's wife, a Jewish girl from Milwaukee, was in law school, and while clerking, she wrote the brief defending a slow dude who picked twenty pounds of ditchweed found roadside. In a simple twist of fate, he threw it into the back of his truck and found himself facing twenty-five years to life. Stoned ourselves one steamy July night after poker, we were outraged as we listened to the story and passed a joint.

Anita was fastidious and neurotic. You could eat off her floors, and she had matching sets of everything, plus a special horse-themed rumpus room and a pug named Nelson Algren. Nelson loved the scent of a woman. He overindulged in stained panties left on the floor, one houseguest learned. A brick on the bathroom wastebasket kept him from feasting on bloody tampons.

Menstruaters make me think of their opposite—the fruitful multipliers (which Dan and Anita and Sue and Eric later became). Raised by a single mom, Nancy was from a family of seven sisters and one brother. With Al, she birthed three fair, angelic boys. She and her tribe of sisters believed strongly in home birth. When one gave birth, all traveled to help that sister, and the event was a mass familial greeting to the newborn instead of a hospital stay. The woman giving birth would be attended by her midwife and sisters, their own children in the room watching and encouraged to asked questions—e.g., "Mom, is she pooping?" "No, Reigny, that's the baby's head."

Sometimes Nancy's husband, Al, would come along. Al had a gentle, dreamy manner, and he was handsome in his non-vain blondeness. I liked Al a lot, and I also liked his art. I never acknowledged my crush, because he was married and I was with Mark. But it was always nice to see him.

Al's dad was a Wisconsin dairy farmer. When Al and Nancy— Teutonophiles—wanted to travel to Germany for their art, Mr. Luft would sell a cow. Nancy was upset once because, when Mr. Luft and his farmwife came to Madison for supper, they went to a meat-and-potatoes restaurant that had every kind of potato side dish imaginable—scalloped, mashed, French fries, home fries, you name it—but they didn't have baked. And that's what Mr. Luft had every night with his supper. She'd chosen the place specifically because of the potato side-dish options and it didn't work out. She was really mad that he made a stink.

Sometimes Nancy's brother Chip came with his querulous Nepali girlfriend, Gita, who was very smart and funny, came from Nepali royalty, and cussed like a sailor. The first time I saw Chip, I was at work at the Majestic Theatre, Madison's repertory house, sitting on my sweetheart's lap, necking in the lobby between shows. Chip burst in with a stack of copies of the radical newspaper he edited, published, and distributed, plopped them on the lit table, and, arm in air, yelled, "Support the revolution!" Then he promptly marched out (and we laughed). That was in college. I got to know him better over poker.

Then there was my corn-fed, earnest post-punk sweetie, Mark Penner. He loved Jonathan Richman and Daniel Johnston, the Gun Club and the Birthday Party, the Clash and the Mekons, Television and Wire, Sibelius and Little Richard—and me, and never so much as glanced at another girl. Loyalty incarnate from Nebraska, he taught me that the state capitol, long and tall with a sewer spewing seeds at its pointy head, was called "the prick of the prairie."

I learned a lot from Mark, including gambling, during our "Western Tour" road trip to the West Coast. The Pixies and Throwing Muses went along for the ride, and the fiery, cataclysmic passion of Wagner powered our non-air-conditioned Dodge Dart over that 100-mile lonesome stretch of arid, flaming highway that is Needles, California, to Barstow, California, otherwise known as hell. Zeitgeist, a punk-rock bike messenger and motorcycle bar, was our first stop in San Francisco, but it's not where I lost my T-shirt. That happened at Vesuvio's in North Beach, where Jack Kerouac and the Beats had once hung, kicking back bourbon. But I didn't know until several weeks later when, after driving home through the salt flats and brine shrimp of Utah, through the dry rolling hills of Montana, through the endless sunny cornfields of Nebraska and by Jack the Chili King with a stop in Iowa, we finally reached Wisconsin, abuzz with the rich, fertile life of Indian summer. It was then that I made the fatal reference to "Vesuvius." I had thought the bar was named for the volcano in Pompeii. Mark corrected me. "You're wrong about the name," he claimed. "It's Vesuvio's."

That seemed like nonsense, so I challenged him. "Wanna make a bet?"

He queried, "Are you sure you want to make a bet over this? Are you sure—are you positive? I know I'm right."

He was wrong for sure, I thought. My answer: "Absolutely. Fifty bucks."

From out of his backpack he pulled a pen clearly marked with Vesuvio's name, phone, and address, blue letters printed on white plastic. Mark had brought it back from the bar as a souvenir, and, though joined at the hip as we were, I hadn't noticed. Examining the pen closely, I spotted an "o" and an apostrophe, and no "u" was to be found. I was flabbergasted; I'd been certain I was right. He made me pay: I had to cough up that cash—and cough I did as I placed a fifty-dollar bill in his cocksure hand. I whined and carried on—he was my boyfriend, after all; he was supposed to indulge me! I was very pissed off. But I learned the meaning of a bet.

Mark's parents were corporate gypsies, descended, on his mother's side, from Bohemians—Czech immigrants—who shot and ate squirrels. On his dad's side, his German Mennonite grandpa, Henry, put up telephone poles across the West. I met Grandpa Henry in an elders' home somewhere on the prairie. He left Mark his TV in his will. He was really nice. But Mark's parents were upset that he was joined at the hip with a Heb-chick, and so was his Catholic-girl/punk-rock sister, who gave me size one panties for Christmas when she knew I was a size eight. Mark also loved to gamble, and wanted nothing more than to elope to Vegas. I did not. He found someone who did.

There was one other thing I learned—I learned to chest my cards, because I was famous for flashing. Everyone would always say, "Chest your cards! Chest your cards!" For me, learning to be careful to conceal my hand was a metaphor for being sneakily cautious *in life*. On indie songstress Sarah Dougher's 2001 album *The Bluff*, the title song explores all meanings of that word (bluff), from jumping off of one to chesting a bad hand while betting like you hold a full house. Like Sue, Eric, Nancy, Chip, and Dan, the song came from Minnesota. Sarah said she was walking with her Minnesotan grandmother in Red Wing, on a bluff high above the Mississippi River, when the song—and album—germinated.

Speaking of Minnesota, the last time I was in Minneapolis, I tried looking up Sue and Eric and their two boys in the phone book. There were thousands of Sue Johnsons and Eric Olsons, alone and combined. Resignedly, I laughed. I was in the land of Johnsons and Olsons. No way was I going to find my Johnson and Olson in the phone book. That was one hand I had to fold.

nothing in moderation– ernie Kovacs and poker

an interview with edie adams

by Jake Austen

Ernie Kovacs and Edie Adams were one of Hollywood's most talented couples. He was a surrealist visionary who pioneered progressive comedy on TV. She was (in addition to being his muse) an angelic singer, and she possessed the rare combination of stunning beauty and killer comedic sensibilities. After applying his zany aesthetics to local radio and TV in Philadelphia, Kovacs moved on the New York and eventually Hollywood. There he spent the 1950s creating innovative television decades before David Letterman figured out how to sell Kovacsian comedy to the mainstream. Though his TV work was only moderately successful commercially, Kovacs was a beloved showbiz figure for many reasons, not the least of which were his legendary, marathon poker games. Kovacs played cards with Jack Lemmon, Billy Wilder, Tony Curtis, Frank Sinatra, and countless Tinseltown types, from the loftiest executives to the humblest crew members. A reckless player (he often tried to buy the pot with crazy betting on terrible hands, and allegedly once won a $48,000 hand

by drawing two for an inside straight) and a big spender, Kovacs was wrestling with severe money troubles when he died in a tragic auto accident at the age of forty-two. But he had lived his life the way he wanted to, and when it came to gambling, as with everything else in his life, Kovacs went all-in. What else could you expect from a man whose tombstone reads, "Nothing in Moderation"? Adams, a star of Broadway and Las Vegas in her own right, spoke of Ernie and his obsessions with poker.

Jake Austen: So Ernie Kovacs loved to play poker.

Edie Adams: With him it was not a choice—he just had to do it. At the time none of us was seeing shrinks, it was not psychological or obsessive-compulsive, it was just "He has this little foible, he likes to gamble." It was funny. When he was starting out in Philadelphia he had this game with Joe Behar, our director, and anybody else that would play with him. They'd go over to our tiny, tiny apartment, eight or nine people to play cards. Not only did they not have a table, they did not have any place to sit. So Ernie took the door off the hinges, and they sat on the floor and played. When we were in New York they came out of the woodwork to play at our home. Playwrights and the best of the Broadway scene would come over—Ernie always had a game going. I said, "Just be sure they're out of here before the kids get up to go to school."

JA: Did you ever get to play with them?

EA: No, I was not allowed near because I was considered bad luck. At the poker table or near anything in Vegas I was considered bad luck because I truly could not understand it. I would see amounts of money being lost and I would see hillsides and diamonds going down the drain, I wouldn't just see a great game. After Ernie died and I would play Vegas they said, "You never gamble!" And I would say, it's not that I have anything against it, it's paying my salary here, but

I just am not a gambling person. They asked, "What if we give you money to play with?"

JA: They wanted the gamblers to see the stars playing in the casino?

EA: Oh yeah, so I'd go down with their money and I would deal, I'd play, I'd do anything, but I couldn't understand it.

JA: In Los Angeles, Ernie would have poker games at your home.

EA: All the time, two- or three-day games.

JA: Whom would he play with?

EA: Everybody at one time or another: Frank and Dean—Frank lived right up the street. There were so many kids at Dean's house that on Saturday mornings when the kids would watch *Road Runner*, he would join Ernie in the den. Dean would gamble, but he wasn't set on gambling; he would come up for peace and quiet. Dick Quine, the director, would be there . . . Eddie Fisher . . . a lot of studio executives. The funniest thing to me was that I would go out to the den and I would recognize the actors but I didn't know anyone else. After Ernie died, whenever I went to the studio I would go to the executive dining room and I'd see all these guys. "Oh, hi, Sam, what are you doing here?" "Running the studio." "Oh, is that what you do?" One guy he played with was a fellow who became a professional player, Joe Mikolas. He was a poker buddy who Ernie decided to use on television. Ernie preferred nonactors and he decided we should use Joe because "He's got a good poker face." On one of the Dutch Masters specials, Joe played the poet laureate who read a poem that Ernie wrote, "Dearth . . . The Lack." It was obtuse and surreal, and it was really funny how he underplayed it.

JA: Did Ernie win or lose?

EA: As I understand it he always lost, but he loved the high and the thrill of gambling and living dangerously. I never liked to live dangerously; I liked to live safely.

JA: I would imagine the way he understood people he'd be pretty good at poker.

EA: Well, the way he played poker. . . . He told me something that I have always lived by: in any negotiation where you don't have any real power, if you are the wild card, that is your *only* power. They might laugh when you talk about doing something, but they know by damn you just might do it. Everyone I know that used to play with him says that out of nowhere he would bet a horrendous amount on nothing. . . .

JA: Like drawing to an inside straight?

EA: Sometimes it would come through. But sometimes it wouldn't. Normally he lost, I hear.

JA: What was his poker room like?

EA: Ernie had a three-story study, with a wine cellar in the lower level and a library in the middle, and the top floor was the den. There was a poker table, a built-in desk, a koi pond, a waterfall, and on the other side was a stretch-out cot if you needed a fifteen-minute nap. He had a walk-in steam room. That is what kept them going during three-day poker games—they would take a break and go to the steam room. I remember one time we went to a movie and came back at ten o'clock. Ernie said, "I'm just going to take a steam," and I went to bed. I woke up at about four in the morning and there was no Ernie and I thought, God, he had a heart attack, he went into the steam room and had a heart attack. So I put on a peignoir and went frantically racing through the house. I threw open the door and there was a huge poker game. So I said, "Oh, oh, I'm sorry, excuse me," and I went back out again. Then I heard Ernie say to the guys, "*Who was that?*" [laughs]

JA: Describe the table they played poker on.

EA: Ernie designed the poker table himself. It's about 5 inches thick, of oak, and it is *huge*. It's on a central pedestal so there are no table legs to get in the way of the players' legs.

JA: What's the surface made of?

EA: Just wood, polished. Not cleanly polished, sort of a rough surface. It's very Kovacsian. Someone said, "It's a great man's den," and Ernie said, "No, it's a great young boy's den."

JA: Was he adamant about people using coasters on the table?

EA: He was pretty loose, but it was built for toughness. It was guy furniture. The stairs that went down had the banister filled with swords.

JA: Certainly no games ever ended in a sword fight!

EA: They had two fist fights out there and I don't know what they were about. Dick Quine and two writers. . . . I never could find out what the story was.

JA: Do you remember any funny poker stories?

EA: I think the funniest one was when he had some of the people over from the East. When we first came out we had an NBC tie line, a direct line between our house and NBC in New York. Herbie Susan was a good friend of ours—he did something called *Wide Wide World*, this is around '58, '59. On that show they would film things in Indonesia, or some other place that no one in America knew where it was. And one day the NBC tie line rang when Herbie and Ernie had been in a game in the den for about two or three days. They said they were looking for Herbie Susan and I said, "Isn't he in Indonesia?" They said, "Yes, we can't find him there, we were wondering if you. . . . " I told them I'd go ask Ernie when he last saw Herbie. So I went out and there was a thing that lit up on his door that said, "Not Now." If there was a big game in progress you just couldn't go in. I knocked on the door and said "I'm sorry, I'm sorry, but I've got the NBC operator on the phone, the boss wants to speak to Herbie. I told them I thought he was in Indonesia." And they were sitting there howling, then Ernie says, "Well-l-l-l . . . if he is in Indonesia then *he is in Indonesia!* You tell them that you are going to try the Indonesia operator and that you'll put her on hold and be right back." So I went back inside and I said, "I think we know where he is in Indonesia." Then I was the operator getting Indonesia on the phone. I don't know what they speak in Indonesia, but I figured we were doing a sketch, so I did my best. I finally plugged them into the line in the den. So now they were in Indonesia, and none of us knew anything about the country, so everyone was making jungle calls and sound effects in the background, and there Herbie was saying he was in Indonesia. He'd say, "The rain has been awful," and they'd all make rain sounds. It was just crazy, the absolute nuttiness of it all. They had just been out there playing poker for three days.

JA: What would they eat?

EA: If there was a game going on, Nan Burris, who cooked for us, knew what each player liked to eat. She worked for everyone: Selznick, Howard Hughes . . . she knew exactly what everyone liked and would have it on the stove. She wouldn't stay up all night for them, but when they wanted something they would go get it, and it would be ready for them. But she knew Mr. Goldwyn had to eat by seven o' clock, if he didn't eat by seven o' clock . . . [laughs].

JA: Who else played?

EA: One of the biggest gamblers was Phil Silvers. Also Robert Wagner. . . . After Ernie died, here comes someone to my front gate, and he said, "Edie, it's Robert Wagner, I have something for you." It was $10,000 he said he owed to Ernie. That was the sweetest thing I ever heard in my whole life. Then I had other people, one socialite from New York who shall remain nameless, who said Ernie owed

$4,500 and wanted it in cash immediately. It was so funny who rallied and who sallied.

JA: You mentioned Phil Silvers. Was he as good at gambling as his act would imply?

EA: No! When he went to Vegas he was told by his manager that he wouldn't get paid—he would get an allowance. In those days you would get paid your entire $25,000 in cash, and then you had to walk through the entire gambling area, which for a gambler is a problem. So he would just get an allowance that he could gamble on for an hour or two, but when that was gone that was it. So he would go and if he would win he would stay out later and later and later, and one time he won *completely* and the guys with him said, "Come on, you're going to bed." He went into the room around three in the morning and he couldn't sleep, he absolutely couldn't sleep. He went back out and gambled and lost his winnings and another $5,000 and he went back and he slept like a baby. [Laughs.] You know what I'm saying, it's a very complex kind of thing. It's depressive, something or another with your brain.

JA: And Ernie was the same way?

EA: Absolutely, he couldn't help it. He was obsessed with poker. I don't believe it's a choice, it's a given. You are born with DNA with something missing. Obsessive and compulsive gamblers, they can't help it. It is in your system.

JA: That said, do you think Ernie enjoyed himself when he was playing poker?

EA: It's the only thing I think he ever really enjoyed to the fullest.

◆ Poker Sympathy by C.M. Coolidge ◆

PRACTICAL AND
IMPRACTICAL TIPS

FLUSHED WITH DRINK

A GUIDE TO POKER GAME DRINKS

by David Wondrich

Nothing goes so well with sin as more sin, a fact acknowledged by the H. Jackson distilling company back in 1914, when they included a free deck of cards with every two gallons of whiskey bought. Now, I'm not saying that whiskey is the only thing to drink when you're playing poker, but it sure is a reasonable place to start. It depends, of course, on your Game Archetype—the ideal poker game upon which yours is modeled. Every game has a GA, whether it be historical, fictional, or even entirely mythical, and different GAs call for different drinks. Here, then, are five of the most common, each with appropriate tipple.

The Alamo Saloon

If your idea of poker heaven is inseparable from sweat-stained Stetson hats and piano players with garters on their sleeves; if you'd gladly swap your rec room for Abilene's Alamo Saloon, where Wild Bill Hickok kept the peace in between hands, there's really only one drink that will do. Bourbon whiskey. Most cowboys were Southerners, and Southerners drank bourbon. Preferably, it should be served in proper Old West style: give each player a glass—for absolute authenticity, one of those small, thick-bottomed things with "church windows," as they used to be known, molded around the base—and pass the bottle around, letting 'em help themselves. It's probably a good idea to give everyone a glass of ice water and to keep a big jug of it on the table.

If the straight stuff is too much of a burden for all or any involved, the next best thing to deploy is the old-fashioned (also known as the old-fashioned whiskey cocktail): place a sugar cube (or ½ teaspoon of granulated sugar) in the bottom of—what else—an old-fashioned glass (or other heavy-bottomed tumbler), hit it with two good squirts of Angostura bitters, add a teaspoon—no more— of H_2O, and muddle it all together with a pestle, wooden spoon, or whatever else you've got handy. Add two ounces of bourbon, stir well, and slip in one or two large ice cubes. Squeeze a strip of lemon peel over the top (when cutting these, aim for ¼-inch by 1-inch strips, and try not to get any of the bitter white pith), drop it in, and serve. Do not add cherry, orange slice, or pineapple stick, no matter what modern bartending guides may say. It's always best to let these sit for three or four minutes before taking the first sip. (Note: everything up to the addition of ice can be done in advance.)

Recommended brands: Old Forester 100 proof, Knob Creek, Wild Turkey Russell's Reserve, something of that ilk. A real hombre or, for that matter, cowgirl, won't touch a whiskey under 100 proof.

The Algonquin

Now, some folks find all that cowboy stuff, well, silly. If your GA involves fast-talking sophisticates cracking wise and taking no prisoners (e.g., George S. Kaufman's Thanatopsis Inside Straight Poker Club, an offshoot of the Algonquin Round Table that was staffed with various *New Yorker* writers, columnists, and other professional wits), then make your whiskey rye, and drink it with ginger ale. Straight rye whiskey, the ancestral drink of the Mid-Atlantic states, can be kinda hard to find these days, but nothing else has that cynical, big-city toughness to it.

For a proper rye highball, drop two ice cubes into a tall, narrow glass (the smaller the surface area of the drink, the longer the bubbles will last). Add two ounces of rye, top off with three to five ounces of chilled ginger ale (deeply traditional, although you can use club soda, too) and stir briefly with something nonmetallic (that's supposed to preserve the bubbles). That's it.

Recommended brands: Wild Turkey Rye, 101 proof (not the same as Wild Turkey Bourbon), Old Overholt, Jim Beam, Rittenhouse 100 proof. If you can't find rye and your local store won't order it, in desperation you can substitute Canadian Club, just like they did during Prohibition.

The Sting

Perhaps your GA involves high-rolling "businessmen" who know how to dress properly and keep their mouths shut—and take their card playing very seriously indeed. Here's where you need to jump across the Pond and bring in some foreign help: Scotch whisky or Irish whiskey, and not the cheap stuff. Straight, no soda. Maybe a splash of water. But let's get back to the game, OK?

Recommended brands: Scotch: single malt, but nothing that will call too much attention to itself—the Glenlivet 18-year-old, Glenmorangie 15, a nice Macallan; if you need more peat, the Oban. Irish: Redbreast or Jameson Gold if you can find them.

Casino Royale

There are certain GAs that do not call for whiskey in any form. Some
of them involve wine, but we don't endorse them. Wine goes with
food. Did you come to eat or play cards? There is, though, one exception. If your poker group is heavily invested in shawl-collared tuxedos and backless gowns; if a member of your group keeps his or her
cigarettes in a case and smokes them with a holder; if a deposed
member of a Balkan royal family, or anyone who wants to be one, is
at the table, you'll need buckets of ice. How else will the champagne
stay cold? (You'll keep the vodka in the freezer, of course, dispens-
ing little glasses of it on demand.)

If you can't afford the best champagne—perhaps there's been a
revolution back home—a champagne cocktail will work wonders
with an indifferent grade of fizz. Simply drop a sugar cube into a
champagne flute, lash it with two squirts of Angostura bitters, add
an ice cube, and fill with cold champagne (or champagnelike substance). Squeeze a twist of lemon peel over the top and drop it in.
Do not stir.

Recommended brands: If theIf royal revenues are really rolling in,
Krug. If not so much, Bollinger. If not at all, Mionetto prosecco is
cheap and not bad. As for vodka—go with Eastern Europe: Stolich-
naya Cristall, Wyborowa, Belvedere (nothing flavored, mind you).

Chez Oscar

If, on the other hand, your idea of a real poker game involves a bunch
of regular guys who manage to get away from the missus and the
ankle biters for a little while and relive the slovenly joys of bache-
lorhood, you know what you'll be drinking. Bud. And what the hell
is wrong with that, pal? That's right, nothing.

tips for chips

some thoughts on poker chips

by Jake Austen

Towers of Power: How to Stack Chips

The way a man handles his poker chips says a lot about him. It certainly says less about him then the way he handles a draw-to-the-inside-straight decision or the way he handles the other players when he's holding "the nuts," but it says a lot nonetheless. And if you handle your chips poorly enough, good opponents will make those chips their own soon enough.

Many tells involve chip handling. Some anxious gamblers palm the big chips too early or too eagerly when in possession of a powerful hand. Some players nervously fondle the chips when they bluff. Some players separate their original stake from their winnings, telegraphing what bets will make them fold.

But poor chip handling is not just a reflection of your skills as a poker player; it is a matter of style. Perhaps we all do not want to be classy when we play poker (Oscar Madison is as valid a card-playing icon as James Bond), but we all want to seem cool, or at least like we know what we are doing. While I cannot offer the perfect way to stack chips—that is a personal decision for each player—I can offer some truly irksome methods that will make you look like a chump any night of the week.

The worst way to stack chips is the non-stack. A big, messy pile of chips is an insult to your opponents and to the game. Stray chips getting too close to the pot or to another player's stack is an inevitability, and stopping game play to argue over the ownership of quarters or dimes is absurd. If you are a mound-of-chips perpetrator, please refer back to your preschool training in the art of stacking. If you need to practice at home with some alphabet blocks, by all means do.

Only slightly better is the precarious skyscraper of chips. We all know what Freud would say about a compulsion to have a massive cylinder of chips in front of you as you test your manhood against a group of dudes (with cigars!). But, following up on that analysis, think of the emasculation you will feel when your obelisk falls over (or when losses reduce it to a tiny stub).

Another problematic stack system is one that would make Kenny Rogers's "the Gambler" character roll over in his grave. While all of us count our money while sitting at the table to some degree, making a show of it or being absurdly obvious is a no-class move. Methodically stacking your chips so that their height demarcates exact denominations (keeping all your ten-cent chips in dollar stacks, all your quarter chips in five dollar stacks, etc.) makes you seem like a gloating jerk if you are ahead, and rather pathetic if you are doing poorly. I once saw a ridiculous guy play behind a sprawling neighborhood of tiny stacks of four twenty-five-cent chips. Trust your arithmetic abilities, people! Even under pressure, I truly believe you will be able to compute on the fly how many quarters there are in a dollar raise!

On the other hand, the thing about tells, tics, and annoying habits is that the crafty player can use his own seeming weaknesses against his opponents. So if you know how to make these chip-stacking faux pas work to your advantage (and you don't mind everyone hating you), more power to you.

Cash Is Clay: Should One Splurge on Fancy Chips?

While plastic chips can certainly do their job, poker is a man's game, and there are times when handling an emaciated checker piece may make you feel a little juvenile. Those are the times to consider the purchase of a grown-up set of poker chips.

Clay chips (which are not actually made of clay, by the way) are the casino standard and can make you feel like a real big shot. Like a major-league baseball or a really good hammer, good clay chips seem to possess the perfect weight and size for their task. Poker junkies will swear they handle better than their acrylic counterparts and that ultimately they can profoundly affect the vibe of your poker table.

You can pay as little as $20 for a small set of 100 clay chips, or you could pay over $1,000 for a full set in a fancy case. Cheaper chips are really just hard plastic filled with "clay," or a lead powder, to get the proper weight (around nine grams). They usually come in solid colors like plastic chips, instead of bearing the intricate designs and patterns available on more pricey chips. You can also get custom chips made with your name or picture or family crest on them. Laying out big money for a set of play money is a big decision, though, and there are a few different factors to consider.

One philosophy for weighing this decision is to apply your hazy memories of freshman-level Econ. Will the cost of these chips be offset by an increase of winnings at poker? Or, alternately, have you won enough to justify such a purchase? If you are playing a friendly game where each week you are up or down five to ten dollars, a $200 purchase isn't going to pay for itself anytime soon, even if it somehow intimidates your opponents, keeps sheep coming back, or makes you play with more confidence. Of course, in a low-stakes game the money is pretty symbolic anyhow; it's really just an escape where you get to live a fantasy by imagining how you plug into the vast, exciting poker underworld. And in these terms, if nice chips will add to the fantasy, so be it. Still, if you keep mental wins-and-losses columns, throwing a few extra Ben Franklins in the red is a tough hit to take.

Also, owning something nice can be a burden. Are you going to be nervous about chips getting chipped (hard to do, but not impossible) or getting dirty (you have to clean them with a toothbrush), and will these concerns take you out of your game? If you paid hundreds for the case, are you always going to keep an eye on it when you should be watching your opponents for tells? Like someone who stops driving because his classic sports car is too nice, you have to be aware of the possible pitfalls of having too posh a possession.

Of course, if you really desire poker with fancy clay chips and do not want to deal with the cost, the solution is simple: invite someone who already owns a set to join your game!

Potato, Chocolate, and Nacho: Thoughts on Nonstandard Chips

In the movie *One Flew Over the Cuckoo's Nest* (1975), Randle McMurphy (Jack Nicholson) engages the ultimate collection of eccentric 1970s characters in a loony-bin blackjack game. The gang is using cigarettes in lieu of ten-cent chips, and all is going well (from hustling Randle's perspective) until fidgety Martini (Danny Devito) breaks one in half to bet a nickel.

Of course, the broken cigarette is worthless. These "chips" represent both the money that Randle bilks the loons out of *and* their value as things you smoke. They are two things simultaneously, an idea that can be confusing to those who never studied the Holy Trinity in seminary school. For that and many other reasons, I do not recommend playing with nontraditional chips.

For example, if you are playing with edible chips, say, peppermint candies or Cheetos, what happens if someone eats one? If the chips actually just represent themselves and you are only playing to increase your intake of Cheetos, then eat away! But if you got the snack food after paying a cash buy-in, or as markers in some credit system, then eating your chip throws everything off. And what if you are playing with seashells, and white shells are a quarter, off-white shells fifty cents, and luminescent white shells a dollar? That can get pretty confusing pretty quick.

If you are in prison or on a deserted island or at summer camp and you are playing hands of poker with pebbles or toenail clippings or popcorn to stave off insanity, that's perfectly acceptable. Otherwise, just get some damn chips.

The Cash Money Crew: Should One Forgo Chips Altogether?

Some players don't see the point of chips at all. If you are playing for money, why not throw real money in the pot? However, in a game that operates in increments of less than a dollar, this often requires the bringing of your own load of change. So now you're an old lady in front of a slot machine clutching her money bucket, or a five-year-old who just cracked his piggy bank. In addition to these non-manly associations, I think there is another serious argument for the superiority of chips in a low-stakes game.

If you are playing a table where significant amounts of money pass between people, and most bets will be made in paper, then playing with cash has some nice aesthetic advantages. If you have a pile of bills in the center of the table, it is only a matter of time before some watches and wedding rings and car keys end up in there, and isn't that the ultimate poker fantasy? However, this isn't going to happen in a nickel-ante game. And of all the arguments for chips instead of change, the most significant one is . . . it ain't poker if there ain't real money. And at some point, when you play with the jingly stuff you are basically betting from your grandma's penny jar and returning the pennies when the game is over.

One night I was playing in a fifty-cent-limit game and amazingly left with $40 in winnings . . . all in change! I might as well have won Confederate dollars, because this money was just worthless. I put it in a jar by the door and dipped into it for train fare or to buy a paper, but I would have had train fare or paper money anyhow. If I win an extra $40 one week I should be able to buy $40 worth of more stuff than I would on other weeks. But I can't buy a $20 meal with dimes and nickels, can't buy a DVD with five pounds of silver, can't pay for drinks at a bar with a sack of change. Had we played with chips and I had cashed out in bills, I would have gotten extra full, entertained, or drunk that week.

So leave the cash for the big boys (who usually prefer chips, anyhow) and take your bulging pockets filled with change to the store to buy a set of poker chips.

HOW to Kick an Unwanted Player out of the group

by Bobby Thomas

As far as poker goes, I think I'm a lucky man. I've played poker with a great group of guys for nearly fifteen years. My wife, who is amazing, doesn't mind my staying out half the night once a week. And on top of that (I'm not bragging here; this is just true), I almost always leave these poker nights a winner. As everyone knows, when you've got something that's going good, you don't want to mess with it. But sometimes change is unavoidable. So when one of the guys moves, another has a kid, and someone else leaves us for a higher-stakes game, and suddenly we're down to four at the table and go three weeks without a high-low game, we look to bring in someone new. I usually keep quiet. It's not my house, and, besides, my wife says that most of my other friends are annoying misfits; in fact, she calls them the "wack pack" and won't let me invite them over to the house when her friends are there. However, I am an integral part of the game (at least I like to think I am), and I've stepped up to do my part to keep our poker night healthy.

And that's where my luck has run dry. On three separate occasions, my pledge has been so unbearable, such a drain on the game, that we've actually had to expel him from the group. This action

does not fit well with the notion of "friendly poker." Worse, since I
was the one who brought them, I felt I was the one who had to get
rid of them. These are people I interact with on a regular basis, and
I was going to have to spend time with them after the banishment.
So, with an "I told you so" from my wife, I handled the situations.
Fortunately, years of poker have made me an expert bluffer, and I
was able to remove these "misfits" as painlessly as possible.

Because I would like to be specific about the nature of these situations and the ways I resolved them, my name and the names of the
unwanted players have been changed.

My first mistake, Gary, I asked to join our game after a longtime
player moved out of town. Gary is a classic type "A" personality. He's
an Arrogant Acerbic Asshole. While I've always known about these
qualities, I also thought they were part of his appeal. He's arrogant,
but he actually is highly intelligent. He talks knowledgably about
musicians, Roman emperors, political conspiracies, meteorology, and
almost all topics. His acerbic sarcasm can actually be kind of clever
and witty. And as far as being an asshole, well, that's why I never
should have let that fucking asshole into our Tuesday night game.

Here's what Gary did. We play fifty-cent limit, and to Gary (a
trust-fund baby) that was somewhat laughable. His reaction to our
low stakes was to raise every round and never fold no matter what
he held. Obviously, he lost what was, for our game, a lot of money.
You might think that splitting thirty or so extra dollars among the
remaining four players would be a good thing, but none of us were
playing fifty-cent limit poker to win our livelihood. We were there
because we liked playing poker. And in order to make low-stakes
poker fun—to make it real gambling—you each have to calibrate
accordingly. Therefore, a maximum has to be treated like a maximum bet, with all the risk, balls-out bravado, and symbolism it
deserves. The first casualty of Gary's antics was the bluff. Since he
never folded or cared about what others bet, you had no chance of
winning without good cards. By raising all bets in all rounds, he also

dragged games out. He changed the timing and nature of every hand. When we tried to tease him out of this annoying habit, he responded with things like, "What's wrong, can't hang?" and "Let's let the cards do the talking." After a month of Tuesdays with Gary, I was given the ax job. Gary had to go.

I'm not saying I handled this nobly. Though I am not always a champion of the "honesty is the best policy" policy, in this case it might have been easier to tell him (a sugarcoated version of) the truth. However, I'm sort of scared of Gary's temper. It sucks to be on the receiving end of one of his lacerating diatribes. So I handled the Gary situation in a cowardly, weak, and, in the end, effective manner. I told him the game was canceled. At first I lied, saying the host would be out of town on vacation for a while. Then I lied again, telling him the game was changed to Thursdays, a night I knew he taught a class. Actually, that was only a half-lie, as the rest of the group was completely willing to switch the night just to get rid of him. Finally, when his semester was almost over, I told Gary the game had officially and completely ended. I skipped one poker night, instead taking Gary to a Tuesday night movie, to make the lie seem real. He talked at length about his poker prowess and the idiosyncrasies of the other players, all of whom he laughed about and called great guys. Ultimately, his feelings were spared by the very arrogance that necessitated his ouster; he simply couldn't imagine that we wouldn't want him in the group!

When I invited P.J. to our game, I opened the door to an entirely different world of problems. Unlike Gary, P.J. wasn't self-absorbed or rude. In fact, P.J. is one of the nicest people I know. But he is also probably the most nervous poker player in the world. I don't mean he was nervous as in cautious and contemplative; I mean he was sweating, nail-biting, and high-blood-pressure nervous. Though non-poker P.J. was usually fairly loose and funny (he once worked as a joke writer for a famous comedian), the combination of money and math (all his betting decisions were made by calculating ratios and

odds, usually out loud) made him into a fidgeting freak. As he ago-
nized over every move, he drummed the table, he chewed paper, he
tapped a beer bottle against his bottom teeth. He crumbled when a
risk failed, and when he won a hand he breathed heavy sighs of relief.
Never joy. Never a celebratory word or a bit of swagger. Only desperate, fatalistic relief. He went to the bathroom twenty times a
night. He knocked over his drinks. His neuroses were infectious, as
his presence at the table began to unnerve us all. After a couple of
months it became clear that playing with P.J. just wasn't any fun.
The rest of the group began to dread poker night, and I even considered not playing anymore just to avoid having to suffer though
P.J.'s infuriating tics. When a couple of the other regulars bailed at
the last minute one Tuesday, we ended up watching a Nets game on
cable instead of playing, and this was long before the Nets were
watchable. At that moment, I realized something had to be done
about P.J.

Getting rid of P.J. was a much more sensitive matter than oust-
ing Gary. It really wasn't his fault that he was a nervous wreck; he
didn't purposely do anything wrong, and he really seemed to appreciate being in the games. But he had to go. It was P.J. or the group,
and no one is more important than the group. This time we colluded
and conspired to make him quit. We all agreed only to call the games
P.J. couldn't stand. Since he compulsively liked to figure the ratios,
we spent the bulk of a night playing convoluted, impossible-to-
calculate games like stormy weather and baseball, with all kinds of
wild cards. The problem was, we didn't really like these games either,
but it seemed worth it if it drove P.J. away. The most unethical thing
we did was deny him his favorite game, hold 'em. None of us would
call it, and when he did we had all agreed (here's the unethical part:
reverse cheating) to fold early no matter what we had, just so the
game ended quickly. We operated like this for two weeks. I was feeling pretty guilty, but I got a call just before I left work on the third
Tuesday. I then heard P.J. (nervously) tell me not to bother picking

him up for the game (I was his ride). He made some kind of excuse, but basically he made it clear that he was no longer interested in playing.

Again, this worked out in the long run. I regularly socialize with P.J., and a year later he admitted to me that he hated playing poker with us. It made him a wreck, and the only reason he stuck around so long was to not hurt my feelings.

Finally, there was Wade. I've known Wade since high school, and he's always been a cheapy. Still, I figured dime-ante gambling to be anyone's idea of an inexpensive night of entertainment. I miscalculated. Wade's penny-pinching ways made for some boring poker. He was player non grata, folding on almost every hand and never winning much when he had good cards, since he bet so conservatively and obviously wouldn't stay in unless he held the nuts or something near it. He wasn't an especially annoying presence, but it was pitiful to watch him fold on a nickel bet before the flop. At this point the host had redone his basement into an elaborate rec room, and we had expanded the group, and if enough people showed we would break up into two groups of four. I didn't have to get rid of Wade, but he was getting on my nerves, and, with my track record, I was starting to feel guilty about bringing him into the game.

I wasn't sure if everyone shared my doubts about Wade, so I decided to handle this one on my own. Besides, Wade was my long-time friend; he never even came in contact with the other players. So I called Wade one weekend and asked him to shoot some hoops with me. We played for an hour or so, and then I explained to him that the Tuesday poker night was a kind of institution, that it had been going on for almost twenty years, and that it had developed a bit of the bureaucracy and regulation of a long-standing fraternity. I told him that he had been coming to the games on a trial basis, and that a majority of the players had voted against his permanent acceptance. I explained that I had argued in his favor, threatened to quit, and cursed them out for their arrogance, but that they had followed

protocol and come to a democratic decision. Wade asked me why
they had voted against his joining, and all I could think to say was,
"They just didn't like you." He said he hadn't done anything wrong,
and I agreed, assuring him that the others were conceited and he was
better off without them. In an odd way, this lie made Wade and me
closer. For a while, as I worked off my guilt, I hung out with him and
we commiserated about the arrogance and cowardice of some people. We played a lot of basketball and eventually joined a Sunday
league together.

My wife tells me to leave new invites to the poker game to the
host. Apparently, I'm a terrible judge of poker personality. I guess I
have poker friends and non-poker friends, and never the twain shall
meet. And though I'm not proud of all my actions, at least, if I have
to, I know how to kick someone out of the game.

THE 100-YEAR POKER GAME

(THE MOST SUCCESSFUL POKER FORMAT EVER?)

by Darrell Ticehurt

I PLAY IN A REGULAR GAME that has been going since 1902! It is the most successful format I have ever heard of for a poker group, so I thought I'd pass it on:

Stakes: No limit, table stakes.

Buy-in: $20. When you fall below $10 you must buy a $20 stack. If you have more than $10 you may not buy a stack. (The limit on chip buys may be the single most important reason for the success of the game. The purpose of the rule is to stop the plungers from plunging too deeply. We have players who have lost for over thirty years who are still playing! If the losses are controlled for the players who have no self-discipline, then they can view the poker as an expensive, but tolerable and enjoyable, entertainment.)

We play every Tuesday according to a rigid schedule: 4:00 to 7:00 P.M., break for dinner, 8:30 to 10:30 P.M. We also play at lunch every Friday, noon to 2:00 P.M., for those who can make it. There are about thirty-five regular players, and at any one session we usually have fourteen to twenty-four players—two or three tables.

We play at a private club and hire a waiter for each session. We drop $1 or $2 from every pot to cover the cost of the waiter and to create a "kitty pot," a large ante for the last hand. Typically in a two-hour session we will have an $80-to-$100 kitty to play for on the final hand. The purpose of the kitty pot is to have a mechanism to pay the waiter, but, more important, it holds the players to a rigid schedule. No one wants to leave early with a relatively large vested interest in the kitty pot. Further, players arriving late must "buy in" to the kitty pot in order to sit down: this operates as a late tax that increases as the kitty pot increases.

Our game is five-card draw, guts to open, or five-card stud. (The format will work with most single-winner games, but split-pot games aren't really as well suited to this format.) Dealer antes $4, and the first dealer is noted. To insure that the antes are equal, the game ends only with the dealer to the first dealer's right. A marker, usually a pocket knife, is thrown into the first pot, and from then on the winner of the pot that contains the knife will become the stud dealer when it is his turn. The knife is placed into the pot when the player who has won the knife deals. This means that, on average, we will play two hands of stud per round, and draw poker the rest of the time. (The marker was introduced when it was noticed that there was a dealer advantage to draw that didn't accrue to stud, and stud wasn't getting dealt enough.)

In general the game starts off with relatively light action. As more money is introduced into the game, the bet sizes do pick up. By the end of the session, bets of $15 are routine, and the occasional $50 bets are made between the big stacks. The final kitty pot can see several hundred dollars in the pot, with initial bets of more than $100 being common.

Money changes hands at the end of the session. The chips are issued by a scorekeeper, who makes a mark by each player's name for each stack purchased. All cash is paid at the end of the game, and we take checks (and even the occasional marker!). If a guest is brought in, the player sponsoring the guest into the game is responsible for guaranteeing that guest's losses. We do allow early departures, but they are rare, and if the scorekeeper or someone wishes to be accommodating, the early leaver who is ahead will get paid. Otherwise, he must ask someone to collect for him at settling-up time. If he is behind, of course, he just pays up. The reason for the rigidity is to insure that the game starts and stops on time. We settle up after every two- or three-hour session. (Because it is often difficult to get out of work at 4:00 P.M. we will reorganize the early game on Tuesday to accommodate any player who arrives before 5:30 P.M., but late arrivals must still pay the kitty-pot tax.)

We have occasional weekend activities, and we publish a weekend schedule at the start of the year. But even a weekend session never has more than a three-hour session before settling up. Sometimes the next session can follow the previous one by only a few minutes, but we play the kitty pot, settle up, and re-form if we want to play longer.

We keep track of everyone's wins and losses for the entire year, and publish them! That is, we publish the winners' exact winnings, cumulative for the calendar year. The losers' exact losses aren't published, but not appearing on the winners' list makes it obvious who is behind.

We have an annual dinner and Calcutta. At the annual dinner, the six biggest winners (pro rata according to money won) sponsor the seven largest losers at a losers' table, covering each individual's losses up to $100. Also, the same six winners pick up the tab for the annual dinner for all thirty-five-plus regular players.

The Calcutta is an important part of the success of the game. Each player is auctioned at the annual dinner, with the other players bidding on each other. The highest bidder pays his bid amount into a player pool and "owns" that player. The player that is owned, however, has the right to buy 50 percent of himself (this is a right, not an obligation: if a player thinks he went for too much money he can decline the purchase). A player may also bid on, and purchase, 100 percent of himself. The cash pool is invested for the entire year, and the interest pays for the scorekeeper, who keeps the accounts and provides twice-weekly lists of the cumulative winnings for each player. At the end of the year, the "owners" of the top six players (not necessarily the players themselves, since a player may decline to buy half of himself) share in the pool—40 percent for first, 28 percent second, etc.

The Calcutta adds a lot of interest to the game, because either a player is in the running for one of the top six payoff positions or the player owns someone else who is. We have found that the top two of three positions usually are not so closely contested, with an early leader going into a "crouch" to hold position, but more often than not, the third or fourth through sixth positions are not decided until the final night!

Overall, we have found that the very top players consistently finish near the top, but there have been significant swings. We had one player who won two years in a row and played at the losers' table the next year! Several other previous-year winners have ended up at the losers' table as well. Some relatively poor players have a hot year and finish "in the money." The swings are really surprising, and would be hard to believe if we didn't keep such careful records.

The game has been played with this basic format since 1902, so we must be doing something right. I think important success factors are the kitty pot, which holds the game to a schedule, and the limit on buys, which stops the big loser from plunging too deeply. We have one player who has lost every year since 1956, but he keeps on playing! The Calcutta adds a lot of interest, but that and the annual dinner are arguably less important.

We have players in the game who have been there since the 1940s. We lose one or two players a year and add that many, so the total number of players has stayed in the thirties for some time. Overall, I have noticed that the "rocks" do well, usually fighting for the fourth through sixth positions, but that the more aggressive players usually win the Calcutta. These more aggressive players can have bigger win/loss swings, however, which is why some winners one year are at the losers' table the next year. The kitty pots contribute to the sometimes wild swings and we do keep track of, and publish, the number of kitty pots won. Usually the very top players and the very worst players lead in the number of kitty pots won!

Also, the number of winners in the game is fairly constant, with about 60 percent of the players in any given year having winnings, however small. And, except for the top two or three winners, the rest of the pack is usually barely above the line, with placings often being awarded to players who have only won a few hundred dollars for the year.

I don't know if this game is the longest-running game ever, but it sure has to be up there! We continue to play the draw/stud format because we don't want to change a winning formula, but I think we would survive the transition to more modern games quite easily.

We even have an occasional social function that includes wives, a good marriage-management philosophy, I think. And a little fun every Tuesday that doesn't create too much of a dent in the checkbook and that gets everyone home at a reasonable hour have made this into a wife's favorite husband's activity.

a (very) Brief Treatise on Poker Snacks

by Jake Austen

WHILE SNACKS are a crucial part of neighborhood poker, I don't believe that one should go to great lengths either to discuss or prepare them. Felix Unger single-handedly killed a longtime neighborhood game by paying too much attention to hors d'oeuvres, so don't fall into that same trap.

There are three basic rules to follow when considering what sustenance to provide to your poker guests.

Rule 1: To quote a Greek philosopher, "Beer *is* food." (The "Greek" philosopher in question was a fraternity dude I met at a state school.)

Rule 2: If you can't wipe it off a card, don't serve it. Potato chip grease, nacho cheese, and salt all can be easily removed from a modern-day plastic-coated card. However, more hazardous materials include hot taffy apples, bubbling fondue oil, and the scarlet-hued sauce/chicken grease hybrid that secretes from buffalo wings.

And finally, **Rule 3:** Just order a pizza.

A few random tips for poker-snack menus: You can't go wrong with chips or popcorn (unless you get caramel corn). Shrimp with cocktail sauce is classy, but not pompous. Phyllo triangles with basil, zucchini, and pine nuts is, in fact, too pompous for poker. Everyone loves chili, but it is a two-hand food, so if you want no stoppage of card play, avoid it. Crudités or other vegetable-based snacks are not insulting to your players' collective manhood, especially if creamy dips are involved. Deviled eggs, bean dip, or other flatulence-inducing delicacies may not be good offerings for a marathon game with guys who think fart jokes are funny (unless you are one of those guys, in which case it is an inspired idea).

WHY YOU SHOULD UNDERSTAND YOUR NICKNAME

by Nolan Dalla

THERE WERE MANY unusual characters back in Dallas during the old days. Every player seemed to have at least one distinguishing feature that made them memorable in some way. Iranian Mike. Troy "the Protector." Doc. Someone called me "Blondie," because I had blonde hair. One player was nicknamed "Rabbit." For the life of me, I have no idea what his real name was—we just called him Rabbit.

Rabbit had a big, bushy white mustache. Anytime he had a good hand his upper lip would start twitching—you know, just like the whiskers on a little bunny rabbit. That twitching white mustache was the most obvious tell you could imagine. So, if Rabbit was involved in a pot and he was twitching, he'd almost never get action. Rabbit never could figure out why nobody ever called his bets. Come to think of it, he must have wondered why everybody called him Rabbit.

A BIG HAND FOR THE LITTLE LADY

Breaking the Gender Barrier

by Elizabeth Rapoport

THE PREVAILING ATTITUDE toward women playing poker was pretty well summed up in an episode of the wildly popular sitcom *Friends*. The twentysomething guys are oh-so-patiently indoctrinating their female friends into the subtleties of the game. "Whaddya need?" Ross asks ditzy Phoebe, preparing to deal her the requested number of cards for five-card draw. "Oh, like, the ten of spades," she replies in typically spacey fashion. "Ooh, ooh, I've got that, you can have mine, I'm not going to use it," squeals Rachel, passing the card. Big eye rolls from all the guys. Dames!

Give me a break. And give me that sibilant slide of the cards, the arched-eyebrow looks followed by the soft clinking of chips, the blue halo of smoke over the table, the elbows crowding out the beer bottles and ashtrays—I want in. Just give me a chance, and I promise I won't disgrace my sex.

I get my chance when a bunch of guys who play every Tuesday lose their sixth. First they try to recruit my husband. After one evening, he comes home broke and bewildered. Seeing my opening, I leverage an acquaintanceship with one of the players and muscle my way to the table. The way I see it, only three concerns dim my prospects.

First, I'm crashing an all-male game; is this OK, or am I prizing a crack in some sacred Old Boy forcefield? (It doesn't help that I'm beer-drinking-impaired—will they freeze me out if I sip Diet Coke?) Second, is that cigar thing an absolute prerequisite? (The smell clings to my sweaters and it's a pain to wash them out.) Third, and perhaps most significant: technically speaking I know jack about poker, unless you're counting a bout of strip in my extreme youth (sadly, this was on a Girl Scout sleepaway). Gamely, I forge ahead.

Weeks one and two are spent redistributing my wealth among my heartless yet surprisingly patient (no other sixth has turned up) fellow players. My nonexemplary play lands me an induction into the "bobo squad." Weary of my extremely short memory, my fellow card sharps tape a neatly printed what-beats-what list next to my chair. Busted.

As I feared, the girl thing is a bit of a damper at first. No one even knows what to do with me when I walk in; a hearty handshake seems falsely jovial, a kiss just feels wrong. I compromise by busying myself with my coat while everyone else takes their seats.

A month into play, I try to cover up a somewhat lame bluff by announcing that I'm wearing my lucky bra. Silence. Then Jon counters by announcing he's wearing women's underwear. Neal informs us he's not wearing any underwear. Amazingly, my bluff succeeds. Soon Neal is sufficiently confident to venture the first off-color joke in my presence—at last, I'm in.

By now I've bought a poker guide and am starting to hold my own. I'm even venturing some patter when it's my deal: "A bullet to the gentleman in the plaid shirt" (said when dealing out an ace); "A small boat, but it'll float" (said when fanning out a full house with no face cards); or "You flaming dirtbag" (said when a completely hidden flush trumps my straight).

As the game rotates from house to house, each night's host is responsible for snacks and beverages. "Geez, I shouldn't be eating this kind of crap," says Dave, hitching up his Dockers after con-

suming a trough of chips, caramel corn, and M&Ms. The most
benign thing I gobble throughout this three-hour food-and-card orgy
is strawberry Twizzlers, which may not, strictly speaking, embrace
any of the food groups. (Months later, Noah admits he's put on
twelve pounds since we started playing; Neal, eight. As we work our
way around the table, I realize that I'm the only one who doesn't seem
to have gained any weight yet, but then I'm guessing I'm the only one
squeezing in a "Buns of Steel" workout before the game.) I'm grateful when Bruce breaks the crudités barrier by serving carrots—
grateful, that is, for an option less calorie-laden than Ring-Ding
snack cakes.

Failure to provide an adequate repast is quickly dubbed "being
snackface." I notice a subtle game of one-upmanship going on at the
sideboard. Not content to measure each other by the size of their
stacks, the guys seem to be competing to see who can offer the greatest variety of beer, chips, and dessert items. One player heaped with
the ignominy of being "snackface" one week (generic cola, stale Halloween candy, no chocolate) battles back the next time by serving
shrimp with cocktail sauce, but is dumped on once again when he
scurrilously tries to retire the platter halfway through the evening.
After months of oscillation, we arrive more or less at equilibrium:
two varieties of beer, two kinds of chips, one chocolate offering, and
the ubiquitous Twizzlers.

Perhaps it's a pathetic commentary on my social life, but these
days I'm practically living for Tuesday nights. For one evening a
week, I leave the office at the office, shift the parental mantle onto
my husband's shoulders (must remember to tip the man next Christmas), and lose myself in the cards. There's no greater high than when
the cards are coming your way and your only job is to bump like
crazy, and no darker shroud than when you have to fold a flush and
surrender huge chunks of chips to that miracle full house.

I'm now at the stage where I have to make a decision about how
serious I want to get about this game. The pile of poker books on

my night stand grows taller by the month, but as soon as an author offers a shortcut for calculating the odds for a given hand (" . . . If one of the three players drops out, your probability of being out-drawn decreases to 44 percent . . . "), I start having an out-of-body experience.

For me, it's not really about fiscal responsibility through chip maximization; it's about staying in stupidly for three rounds on the wild chance that I'll snag the monster hand in the fourth that will crush the uncrushable Jon. I don't need probabilities to enjoy the mind games that come from second-, third-, and fourth-guessing a bunch of regulars who have burnished their perceived playing patterns to a high finish, the better to bluff you with, my dear. My costliest hand was actually my most satisfying: the bold and failed bluff actually earned me a round of respectful applause from the table.

Now and then we recruit an outside player to round out the game. When my neighbor Gary steps up to the plate one night, it becomes tragically clear that he has misread his hand and cannot win, although he is raising the maximum with each round. I know I have him beat. My only question is, do I go easy on him out of pity—his is a fundamental misunderstanding of the rules, not a mere miscalculation—or do I bleed him? And if I really nail him, will he retaliate by revoking his daughter's babysitting license at our house? I adhere to the poker code of honor and drain him dry.

Another time, Gary's wife, Sherril, fills in. She proves an able and affable player, but nonetheless her stack of chips drains away as the night wears on, many of them coming to rest in front of me. I'm raising her again and again—hard. There's something about her playing style that's making me just a bit more aggressive than need be. It's not until the next morning that I realize what the problem is: Sherril is prettier than me.

Poker has so subsumed my psyche that I'm now compelled to translate everything in life into its terms. Surprise: in one of those satisfying instances in which life is breathed into a cliché, I discover that it really isn't so much the cards you're dealt, but how you play them. I'm a better negotiator on the job because I'm a better bluffer and a better folder. I babble on about the game to all my coworkers and fetishize one who's been playing in a high-stakes game for decades. I hope my friends have more stomach for this latest obsession than for my tennis-as-a-metaphor-for-life phase, or my even more regrettable cute-shoes-as-life phase. When my husband presents me with my own monogrammed chips for my birthday, I feel he has touched my sensuous core as surely as if he'd given me a teddy.

Tradition dictates that I now relate my incredible poker prowess, how after a slow start I regularly kick poker butt, leaving a trail of slack-jawed yet admiring guys in my wake (take that, Phoebe). In fact, after almost a year of weekly play, I'm probably just about breaking even. Through some karmic wrinkle, I am currently the record holder for a single night's winnings, though in our circle that doesn't even carry into the three digits. Ours is a middling-stakes game—a nice win and I'll feel flush enough to order a couple of double-tall lattes the next day, but I won't be springing for dinner at Lutèce. (I simply deduct my losses from the kids' college funds.)

But as in all good neighborhood poker, winnings are beside the point. I'm just happy to be one of the guys.

toward an aesthetic of music for poker (plus a few tips)

by Yuval Taylor

Axiom. The musicians on your sound system are the players at the next table. Their game and yours are symbiotic.

Corollary #1. Since the ideal number of poker players in a game is between five and seven, quintets, sextets, and septets are ideal for your sound system. (Poker can, of course, also be played by three, four, eight, or nine people; but music made by one, two, or more than ten people is not recommended.) If you like classical music, Mozart's string quintets are immensely enjoyable. If you like jazz, I suggest the Henry Threadgill Sextett [*sic*], who recorded a number of excellent albums in the 1980s, but there are hundreds of other great groups of this size. If you like rock, one example (out of thousands) is the Mekons, who have been around since the late 1970s in various five-, six-, or seven-member configurations. (Unfortunately, rap music doesn't have a lot of groups of this size, but here are a few: Grandmaster Flash and the Furious Five, the Cold Crush Brothers, Stetsasonic, NWA, Digital Underground, the Roots, and Jurassic 5.) What's nice about these ensembles is that the players contribute almost equally to the proceedings. Groups dominated by one person, such as Bruce Springsteen's E-Street Band, aren't nearly as convivial.

Corollary #2. "Background music," be it muzak, easy listening, smooth jazz, ambient, new age, or LaMonte Young, is entirely inappropriate for poker games. Playing background music is like playing one-armed poker: no conviviality, no esprit. Background music should be reserved for visits to elevators, supermarkets, dentists, prison cells, insane asylums, and hell.

Corollary #3. Poker is a game of deception; therefore, avoid music that strips away all artifice, leaving the musicians naked, honest, and exposed (e.g., Neil Young's *Tonight's the Night* or Percy Sledge's "When a Man Loves a Woman"). Most good music, though, *pretends* to be honest but is really all bluff. Ray Charles can convince almost anyone that he's drowning in his own tears; but really, folks, he's not.

Corollary #4. The music for a good poker game, like a good poker game, is played according to established rules but with plenty of luck, passion, and ingenuity mixed in. Avoid long, formless music with very few rules, like John Coltrane's *Ascension*. On the other hand, some composers, like György Kurtág and John Cage, envision some of their pieces as games; Bach's music is also gamelike, as is that of the rock group XTC, sound pioneer Brian Eno, and many of John Zorn's ensembles. But are these poker games or games of solitaire? Games of pure chance or of resourcefulness and skill? I'll leave that to you to decide.

Corollary #5. Poker playing is elastic. Players fold and bluff, come late and leave early, go broke or get rich, remain unflappable or get hot under the collar. But no matter what, they play together. Music for poker should be equally elastic, equally together. Don't put on

music that is as tight as clockwork, with no wiggle room (e.g., Devo
or the Raymond Scott Quintette). Don't put on music in which one
player hogs the spotlight, taking eleven-minute solos while the others go through their paces.

Corollary #6. Avoid music by people who aren't *play*ful. Brahms,
for instance. Or Joy Division.

Corollary #7. Poker requires a modicum of skill. Avoid musicians
who have little or none (e.g., The Shaggs, John Lee Hooker, the Sex
Pistols, Puff Daddy, or Kenny G.).

Corollary #8. No symphony orchestras, no thirty-piece jazz bands,
no operas, no arena rock, no disco, no techno, no military bands. I
don't care if you're a huge fan of Wagner, Donna Summer, Sousa,
Aerosmith, Moby, or Stan Kenton. The musicians on your sound system are in your *house*. Keep them there.

Corollary #9. Jug bands. Cuban conjuntos. Chamber jazz. Chamber
music in general. Hot fives, sixes, and sevens. Western swing. Rockabilly. Honky-tonk. New Orleans R&B. Soul. Funk. Rock 'n' roll.

◆

Miscellaneous tip #1. Volume. Not so loud that it drowns out anything anyone says. Not so quiet that you don't notice when the
record's over.

Miscellaneous tip #2. Plan ahead. Make a playlist at least as long
as your poker game. (Mix tapes are great; so are programmable CD
players that can hold several CDs at once.) Decide what you're going
to play and in what order *before* your guests arrive. And *never* put
on a record that one of your guests brings you, not even if you've

heard it before. That just encourages other guests to bring *their* records, and before you know it, your guests will be voting on what music to play. Poker is not democratic; neither is music.

Miscellaneous tip #3. If you play with suspicious people, or if you cheat, do not play music by the Who. Their songs ("I Can See for Miles," "Pinball Wizard," "Substitute," and "Magic Bus," to name a few) are all about people whose abilities, were they applied to poker, would result in certain and speedy defeat of all their opponents.

Miscellaneous tip #4. If you have no electricity, it's better to hire live musicians than to rely on a victrola. While victrolas aren't usually as loud as real musicians, they're still pretty damn loud, and you'll spend almost all your time turning records over (they only last three and a half minutes per side), changing needles (every two sides to be safe), and cranking the machine (ditto). Live musicians are more expensive, and you'll need to serve more drinks; on the other hand, you can always win back some of their wages by enticing them to join your game during their breaks. (Player pianos are another option, but those are in limited supply these days; they're also rather inelastic: see Corollary #5.)

ten tips for dealing with cheaters

by Jake Austen and Jason Lutes

CHEATING IS CONSIDERED by some to be just another part of the game. But at a table where everyone is supposed to be friends and an evening's winnings wouldn't treat a family of four to McDonald's, cheating is more than just dishonest . . . it's downright tacky! Here are a few pointers on what to look for and what to do if you suspect dirty dealings at your neighborhood gambling get-together.

1. Keep an eye out for chip shenanigans. It is pretty unlikely that, at your low-stakes neighborhood game, a sophisticated card sharp is going to use near-superhuman sleight of hand to relieve you of your five dollars. It is much more likely that if you get six men together, at least one of them will be a low-down rat bastard. Probably the most common cheating in home games is manipulating chips so the cheater ends up with a few extra dollars at the end of the night. This type of dishonesty is lowly, petty, and hard to detect. One method of chip chicanery is to "splash the pot" (throwing instead of placing chips) and tossing in too few chips. Another opportunity for a scoundrel to steal is when he wins a split pot and offers to do the splitting. A sloppy chip owner who makes piles instead of stacks can fall victim to a lowlife who slyly merges parts of the honest slob's

pile with his own. And the lowest of the low is the cad who buys the same brand of chips at the store, then slips a few into his pile before cashing out early, leaving the last cash-outers to argue over what is perceived to be a problem of poor arithmetic. The only way to counter these actions is to catch a cheat in the act, which is hard to do and harder to prove. But since only the most unpleasant asshole would engage in this kind of trickery, I say you just accuse him boldly and let him quit the game. Even if you're wrong, at least you got rid of the asshole.

2. Watch out for marked cards. It takes some devious preparation for a cheater to get a marked deck of cards into a game, and it is hard for the cheatees to detect tiny differences in the intricate design on the back of the card or to notice a card has been slightly shaved on its side. However, most card marking is not done with specially prepared decks, but is actually done during the game. People alter cards with indentations, with pin-pricks, with special ink or paint they keep hidden from view, and even with condiments or grease from the food served. People bow the card slightly, bend the edges, or use razor-sharp fingernails to leave scratches and dings that only they know to look for. You have one advantage over anyone marking cards during home poker; if they were any good at it, they wouldn't be in your sorry-ass game. Look for the would-be cheat to make rookie mistakes. For example, the cheater in this illustration overdid it. He made the mistake of bringing a deck with previously marked aces (note the discoloration on the card on the left) and then bending all the kings, indenting the jacks, pin-pricking the queens, and splotching mustard on the tens. While a ten-ace straight will win a lot of hands, this kind of overkill will leave a lot of crooks eating knuckle sandwiches.

3. Another method of cheating, which is not unheard of at neighborhood games, is collusion. If two people at a six-chair game are
giving each other signs and merging their winnings at the end of the
night, they are destined to win far more than 33 percent of the hands.
Most tables do not let husbands and wives play at the same time for
this very reason. And if you let a couple play and the results don't
seem to indicate collusion, look around the table again. These are
the wife's husband's buddies . . . if she's cheating on him, it likely is
with one of these guys (if she was cheating with anyone else, she'd
be doing it on her husband's poker night). Perhaps she's teaming up
with her boyfriend to really stick it to the cuckold. Domestic unrest
conspiracy theories aside, here's a few ways to fight poker collusion.
Listen for possible code words like "I forgot to *flush* the toilet," and
"Anybody see that movie *Three Kings*?" Keep alert for the telltale
kick under the table. And if your bankroll is being depleted because
two other players are raising each other to the rafters, and you calculate that the best hand possible for one of the raisers is two pair,
sevens over fours, you may have located your cheaters!

4. You don't have to mark the cards to control the action. One sleight
of hand to watch out for is the stacked deck. Master cheaters can
look at the up cards in the muck (discards) from the previous hand,
and then arrange the cards, and control the shuffle, so that they know
what folks will get in the next deal. This superpower is far rarer than
that of a cad just preparing a second deck beforehand, with the cards
in a certain order. When the time is right he makes the switcheroo
to the sure-win deck (in which he also arranged for other hands to
be awesome, so that everyone bets high before losing to his unbeatable cards). For this to work, the dastardly villain needs to have the
same brand of cards as your table's. Thus, the counter for this move
is always to play with the most off-kilter, obscure souvenir deck of
cards imaginable. If the con man is able to procure a duplicate deck

of your Randy Travis Fan Club or Wisconsin Dells Biblical Gardens Wax Museum playing cards, then he deserves to win.

5. Though really fancy card control isn't too prevalent at low-stakes tables, sometimes people cheat just for practice, or because it's kind of cool to try to manipulate cards. Dealing from the bottom or dealing seconds might not feel like cheating to the cheater. It's more like demonstrating a skillful trick. As opposed to stacking a deck or controlling an entire deal, it is much easier for a cheater just to make sure he will get one card that can drastically improve his odds. For example, if the dealer knows he has a two coming, he will call deuces wild. Dealing from the bottom is literally dealing cards from the bottom of the deck, and if the top card is the one you need, you can deal that to yourself properly. Dealing seconds is pushing two cards out with your thumb from the top of the deck (an honest man would only push one), then retracting the top one while dealing the second. These both look really normal, but if you are intently looking, you can usually detect either transgression being perpetrated. But no need to make the ugly act of forever banning a rogue from your table a totally negative experience! Why not ask the outlaw if he knows any other magic tricks he can demonstrate for the group before his blacklist takes effect. It might make for an exceptionally entertaining banishment!

6. Another common type of cheating in home games is for one player to look at a neighboring opponent's cards, because the crowded table or the angles of seats makes doing so possible. If you notice this, the best counter is to offer loudly, "Hey, stop looking at my fucking cards!"

7. One of the classic cheats is the introduction of extra cards; a fifth ace at the right moment may be dangerous, but it can be pretty lucrative as well. From the cowboy days through the first half of the twentieth century, serious cheats were known to employ mechanical devices that delivered and withdrew cards up their sleeve. As ingenious as these devices are, they are actual fairly easy to detect. Since the majority of these gizmos were built between the 1870s and the Great Depression, even the best-maintained models show some signs of wear. Listen for the whirring of tired gears or the creaking of rusting hinges and joints during gameplay. Of course, a handy cheat can overcome some of these shortcomings with proper maintenance, but in those cases the odor and sleeve-stains caused by WD-40 can usually be detected. Make a clever remark about "elbow grease" as you give the cheat the bum's rush.

8. It is universally acknowledged that one should not play with anyone wearing sunglasses. There is a common method of cheating whereby cards are marked with colored symbols that are only viewable through blue-tinted glasses. My personal take on this is that anyone who wears sunglasses inside, at night, with company over, is not my kind of people. Cheating aside, I'd pass on the game just to avoid spending four hours with a dickhead.

9. Basically, if the new guy can do that trick where the cards fly a foot in the air from one hand to another, looking like an accordion's bellows, it might be a good idea to take a pass on the game. And don't play with anyone dressed as either a nineteenth-century riverboat dandy or a magician. And though I can't give an actual reason why, I'm pretty sure you don't play with *anyone* wearing a monocle!

10. Perhaps the best way of dealing with cheating at a friendly game is via sympathetic indifference. No matter how much he or she may win, anyone who cheats at a nickel-ante poker game is clearly the biggest fucking loser at the table.

♣

HOW TO PLAY POKER WITH THE BOSS

by Eric Ottens

A YEAR AND A HALF AGO I was employed as a corporate lackey, and some coworkers and I had fallen into a weekly schedule of poker at my apartment. Near the end of my employment, one fellow, whom we were aiming to cut from the group because he was kind of a doofus, invited the head of our department to the game. Of course, he accepted.

I didn't like the guy, plus he was my direct superior in the office, so I decided to make the most out of what I saw as a bad situation. Here is my strategy and how it played out. I hope it may be of some use to anyone else who finds themselves in a similar situation.

First, the environment: I wasn't that terribly well paid, but I did have a few nice things, and I decided to hide them. I'd like to say it was so my boss couldn't steal them, but it was more to present myself in the most overworked, underpaid manner possible. I shoved about half of my CDs and DVDs in my closet (though I did leave *Office Space* conspicuously visible), and to make myself look like the well-organized person I pretended to be at work, I even did the dishes and emptied the trash.

Next, the good time: I loaded up on beer. My goal was for everyone to drink a lot, on the premise that people have fun and bond by drinking together. And since I wasn't out to rook anyone, I could afford to compromise my cognitive ability a bit.

Well of course my boss was the first guy through the door. What do you talk about with your boss outside of the office? Inevitably, work. Thankfully the others soon arrived, and we sat down to play. I passed out beer. We played with quarters, a three-raise limit, $2 max per round. It's actually fun to pay attention to this kind of social situation. I'm not sure if people were intentionally watching their language or not, but I noticed that no one swore until after our boss set precedent in a story about his fucking lawn care servicemen.

Anyway, things went well throughout the evening. Beer was consumed and our boss was down quite a bit. Though there was definite concern about beating him too badly, fortunately no one was noticeably in the lead, so there was a nice diffusion of blame. During one of the last few hands everyone else was betting aggressively. I folded early. Bossman was nearing the end of his quarters. On the last round he picked them up, raised the full $2 and dropped his money into the pot. Everyone stayed in, and our boss won the hand with a full house.

The next day three of us were out getting lunch and one of my coworkers started with, "I don't want to talk shit," so I knew it was going to be good. "On that last hand did anyone else notice [our boss] was a quarter short?" My other coworker nearly choked with excitement, "Yes! Yes! I thought that too, but I didn't want to be the one to bring it up!"

Since I folded early I had pretty much quit paying attention, but I was willing to give the guy the benefit of the doubt. Why short-change us by a quarter? I put forth that the most likely explanation was either that my coworkers were mistaken or that our boss had simply made an honest mistake. But these guys would not shut up about it—to the point that, when I quit a month or so later, they actually badgered me until I promised to ask our boss. I already had a new job, I didn't need the reference, and I thought it'd be kind of fun. How did I ask? In the most nonconfrontational way possible: via e-mail, of course. Well, let me tell you, he reacted none too kindly—he went as far as to call me up and leave a screaming, swearing message on my machine.

I told my former coworkers he admitted to the theft and would be reimbursing them twenty-five cents each.

How do you play poker with your boss? Drink a lot. And don't confront him if you think he's cheating.

a pair of shit in hell

by Richard Meltzer

I HAVEN'T PLAYED or even thought about this in seventeen, eighteen years, so let me see if I can reconstruct the specifics . . . it was a *good 'un*.

In the early to mid 1980s, before he turned it into a cable-TV circus, Art Fein hosted a string of poker whatsems at his Hollywood digs that were, well, friendly as all fucking heck. With a core of regulars that included Sam Graham and Paul Body (hi, Paul!), and occasionals like Chuck E. Weiss and Dave and Phil Alvin, the games were for ultra-low stakes, half a step up from pocket change. Since none of us could play worth a ding-dang goddamn, that seemed the way to go.

Until one Sunday night, when these two sharpies Art invited cleaned everybody out in half an hour, none of the players ever took the whole thing too seriously. The winning/losing, the "ritual"—it was just something to accompany the beer, the popcorn, the blah blah blah.

In retrospect, what was most remarkable about these get-togethers was how tolerant people tended to be of each other's cheesy choice of games, both standard and invented. Lotsa times a night, hands would get dealt of cutesy bullcrap like pass the trash, Texas hold 'em, and seven stud with all sorts of dumb things wild, but rarely did anyone spit, cuss, or even wince.

In this miasma of cheesy and dumb, I came up with a game that actually had some viability, one that nobody seemed to mind too much at all: a pair of shit in hell. The object of this five-stud hoot was to make a pair with your hole card—i.e., the *highest* pair utilizing a hole card would win (two competing pairs in a single game only happened maybe twice). The rest of what you had in your hand was irrelevant . . . four aces wouldn't win if they were all exposed.

If nobody made a hole-card pair in a given hand, the pot would remain and you'd deal again until one or more people finally got a proper pair. (Obviously, you could bet outrageously and bluff the rest of the table into dropping out.) Though I don't remember exactly, I assume that if two players got the *same* pair (two pair of nines, for instance), the remainder of their hands would IN THIS CASE ALONE determine the winner, but in all the times we played (twenty? thirty?), this never occurred.

Why nobody hated pair of shit I've got no idea. Less dumb and cute than pass the trash? Dunno. But try it some time, OK?

DIVIDED BY CARDS

AMERICA AND GREAT BRITAIN, POKER VERSUS BRIDGE; OR WHY THE BRITISH PREFER BRIDGE

by David Quantick and Karen Krizanovich

WHEN WE THINK of Americans playing cards, the image is one of hard-bitten gamblers with cheroots between their pursed lips, wearing derby hats, glowering a lot—and playing poker. But what image comes to mind with the British and cards? A lot of toffs in tuxedos getting drunk on port and playing bridge.

The two games divide the United States and United Kingdom more firmly than the cold gray Atlantic Ocean. Apart from the fact that it's hard to imagine America embracing a game whose central technical term is "rubber," there's also the fact that Americans pride themselves on the democracy of American life, and bridge—with its arcane rules, slothy pace, and apparent deep association with nobs—is about as democratic as the Holy Roman Empire. It's no accident that bridge is the game they play in that supertoff movie *Gosford Park*; and quite probably, had they had the time, Hugh Grant's biggest floppy hit movie would have been called *Four Weddings, a Funeral, and a Damn Good Game of Bridge*.

And the British encourage this. Poker, with its associations of gambling, roughness, and card sharpery, just isn't top drawer. "Have you ever seen anyone playing poker in black-tie?" says a snooty friend. "Bridge is too complicated for the lower classes." The friend goes on to explain that Brits' attachment to bridge is all "part of that fabulous holding-on to what separates the upper classes from the masses," before drinking a glass of peasant's blood from a golden top hat. "Also, poker is wonderfully American. It's totally individually competitive, you go out to win for yourself. Bridge is about partnership and teamwork which, as we know, the Americans are not quite so hot at."

As thousands of Americans race to Heathrow Airport, demanding instant repatriation, our friend concedes, "Why stay up all night if you have to share your winnings and the glory?" and "Could you ever see Robert Redford and Paul Newman in *The Sting* playing bridge? No way. It is just not cool, man."

And there we have it. British card players are too greedy and too uncool to play poker. They lack individualism, having had it beaten out of them in the grimy changing rooms of several major British schools. And poor people might get in on the act. Sounds logical to us. However, while we find this truth an alluring one, we suspected that more and deeper truths lay elsewhere, so we asked someone else. And he said, "Poker is about beating the other players. Winning is everything. Bridge is a much more tactical-thinking and skillful game. However good or bad your hand may be, the skill is how you play the hand, not just beating the other players."

We're not sure how true this is. Poker not a game of skill? True, it's somewhat money-oriented, but to suggest that all poker players care about is getting a good hand and going home rich seems a little simplistic.

Our friend goes on. "In poker you play for yourself," he says sternly. "In bridge you play with a partner. A much more sociable game."

Well, true. But you can always cheat at poker and have a friend help you. So how about this?

"Any idiot can learn the rules of poker in a few minutes. Bridge takes a lifetime to learn how to play properly. In poker, you have to guess what the other person is doing through body language, patterns of bidding, and bidding history," our friend asserts. "In bridge, you have to communicate with your partner through a complex process of bidding your hand according to different conventions."

In other words, poker is an exciting system of intelligent interaction and organic reactive thought. Bridge is a cross between joining the Masons and learning a rule book the size of the San Francisco telephone directory.

Finally, before our friends went off to shoot some elephants for fun, they told us, "Bridge is about skill, cooperation, and finesse. It's not just about winning, but about playing well. Poker is about money, aggression, machismo. It's not just that you win, it's that the other person loses. Humiliate the other players."

And that's a bad thing?

♣

♣ A WIFE'S TALE

By Golus & Welch ©

POKER NIGHT AT YUVAL TAYLOR'S HOUSE, HELD EVERY OTHER WEDNESDAY, HAS A CERTAIN GLAMOROUS, NOSTALGIC, ASPIRATIONAL EDGE. THERE ARE NO SIX-PACKS OF PABST BLUE RIBBON, NO BEER NUTS OR 99-CENT POTATO CHIPS, NO SAUSAGE, BOLOGNA OR PICKLES, NO CHEAP CIGARS.

WITH THE DOGGEDNESS OF A WEDDING PLANNER, YUVAL PAINSTAKINGLY RESEARCHES AND HUNTS DOWN THE INGREDIENTS FOR EACH EVENING'S FEATURED DRINK: OBSCURE, HISTORICALLY ACCURATE CONCOCTIONS LIKE HOT BUTTERED RUM, FISH HOUSE PUNCH (AN AMERICAN DRINK DATING FROM 1732), CLOVER CLUBS (A PRE-PROHIBITION FAVORITE), OR MAI TAIS (THE ORIGINAL 1944 VERSION).

THERE'S A CERTAIN GLAMOUR TO THE PLAYERS AS WELL: ARTISTS, WRITERS, MUSICIANS, MISCELLANEOUS KEEPERS OF THE CULTURE TRUST— OCCASIONALLY SOME OF NATIONAL RENOWN, LIKE RADIO HOST IRA GLASS OR CARTOONIST CHRIS WARE.

BUT NO WOMEN.

KAREN

IT'S TOTALLY GUYS, SAYS YUVAL'S WIFE KAREN DUYS, AN ASSISTANT PROFESSOR AT THE UNIVERSITY OF CHICAGO. FEMALE PLAYERS ARE NOT EXPLICITLY BANNED FROM THIS MANLY PURSUIT, BUT THEY AREN'T EXACTLY WELCOMED, EITHER.

WE DID HAVE ONE WOMAN OR TWO COME A FEW TIMES, BUT BECAUSE IT'S MOSTLY GUYS, I THINK IF A WOMAN COMES SHE FEELS A LITTLE ALONE.

WHERE IT ALL HAPPENS... METAL AND GLASS DINING/POKER TABLE

← keep your money to yourselves ladies

KAREN NEVER PLAYS. WHILE THE GUYS STARE EACH OTHER DOWN AT THE KITCHEN TABLE, SHE STAYS UPSTAIRS WITH THE CHILDREN, THALIA, 5, AND JACKIE, 14 MONTHS.

"I'M REALLY NOT A GAME PERSON. I REALLY AM NOT. I DON'T REALLY GET IT. BUT YUVAL LOVES PLAYING GAMES — SCRABBLE, CARDS.

"**U**PSTAIRS IS MY LITTLE SANCTUARY. NONE OF THE POKER PLAYERS GO UPSTAIRS — THEY USE THE BATHROOM IN THE BASEMENT. I DON'T FEEL WEIRD AT ALL IF I COME DOWNSTAIRS, IN TERMS OF GENDER BOUNDARIES OR ANYTHING LIKE THAT, BUT DOWNSTAIRS IS DEFINITELY THE SOCIAL SPACE."

YUVAL'S MALE HEIR JACKIE SEEMS TO LIKE GAMES TOO!

FASCINATING BALL GAME

THALIA PLAYS WITH POKER CHIPS. IT'S FUN!

YUVAL, WHO LOVES PARTIES AS MUCH AS HE LOVES GAMES, INITIALLY INVENTED POKER NIGHT ABOUT THREE YEARS AGO — PARTLY BECAUSE KAREN'S DEMANDING JOB CRIMPED HIS SOCIAL LIFE. "HE'S VERY SOCIAL, WHILE I'M MUCH MORE OF A HOMEBODY. SO THIS WAY I GET TO STAY AT HOME, AND HE GETS TO BE SOCIAL, ALL AT THE SAME TIME.

"**I**T STARTED OUT THAT IT WAS TOTALLY YUVAL'S THING: 'DON'T WORRY, I'LL CLEAN UP THE KITCHEN, I'LL CLEAN UP AFTER THE GAME, IN THE MORNING YOU WON'T EVEN KNOW WE HAD IT.' IT WAS LIKE THAT FOR A LITTLE WHILE. BUT THEN HE STOPPED CLEANING UP THE GLASSES. AND THEN IT WAS THE DINNER DISHES DIDN'T QUITE GET FINISHED, SO THEY WERE LEFT IN THE MORNING. AND NOW I AM INSTRUCTED TO FINISH THE DINNER DISHES WHILE THEY START POKER. IT'S TAKEN A DECIDEDLY BAD TURN."

STILL HAVING FUN.

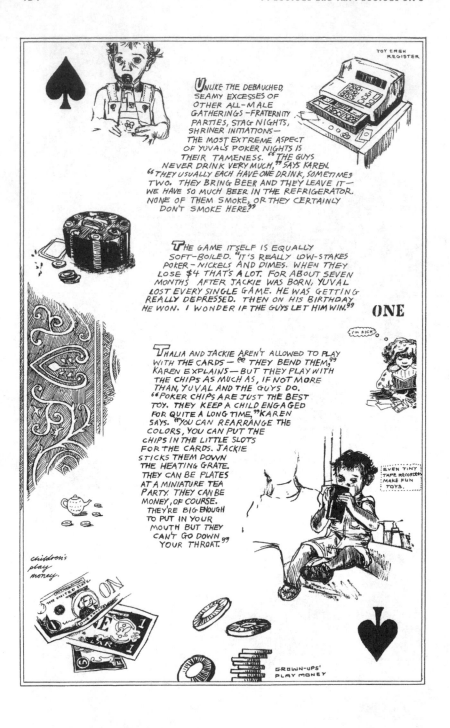

UNLIKE THE DEBAUCHED, SEAMY EXCESSES OF OTHER ALL-MALE GATHERINGS — FRATERNITY PARTIES, STAG NIGHTS, SHRINER INITIATIONS — THE MOST EXTREME ASPECT OF YUVAL'S POKER NIGHTS IS THEIR TAMENESS. "THE GUYS NEVER DRINK VERY MUCH," SAYS KAREN. "THEY USUALLY EACH HAVE ONE DRINK, SOMETIMES TWO. THEY BRING BEER AND THEY LEAVE IT — WE HAVE SO MUCH BEER IN THE REFRIGERATOR. NONE OF THEM SMOKE, OR THEY CERTAINLY DON'T SMOKE HERE."

TOY CASH REGISTER

THE GAME ITSELF IS EQUALLY SOFT-BOILED. "IT'S REALLY LOW-STAKES POKER — NICKELS AND DIMES. WHEN THEY LOSE $4 THAT'S A LOT. FOR ABOUT SEVEN MONTHS AFTER JACKIE WAS BORN, YUVAL LOST EVERY SINGLE GAME. HE WAS GETTING REALLY DEPRESSED. THEN ON HIS BIRTHDAY HE WON. I WONDER IF THE GUYS LET HIM WIN."

ONE

I'M RICH

THALIA AND JACKIE AREN'T ALLOWED TO PLAY WITH THE CARDS — "THEY BEND THEM," KAREN EXPLAINS — BUT THEY PLAY WITH THE CHIPS AS MUCH AS, IF NOT MORE THAN, YUVAL AND THE GUYS DO. "POKER CHIPS ARE JUST THE BEST TOY. THEY KEEP A CHILD ENGAGED FOR QUITE A LONG TIME," KAREN SAYS. "YOU CAN REARRANGE THE COLORS, YOU CAN PUT THE CHIPS IN THE LITTLE SLOTS FOR THE CARDS. JACKIE STICKS THEM DOWN THE HEATING GRATE. THEY CAN BE PLATES AT A MINIATURE TEA PARTY. THEY CAN BE MONEY, OF COURSE. THEY'RE BIG ENOUGH TO PUT IN YOUR MOUTH BUT THEY CAN'T GO DOWN YOUR THROAT."

EVEN TINY TAPE RECORDERS MAKE FUN TOYS.

children's play money.

GROWN-UPS' PLAY MONEY

WHILE NO WOMEN PLAYERS ARE EXPECTED TO MUSCLE INTO THE GAME ANYTIME SOON, IN THE LAST FEW MONTHS THE GROUP HAS ACQUIRED A REGULAR NON-PLAYING FEMALE GUEST: THALIA.

"IT'S A SPECIAL TREAT," SAYS KAREN. "SHE HAS TO EAT DINNER WELL, AND THEN SHE CAN STAY UP TO SEE DADDY'S POKER PALS. SHE HELPS SET UP THE CHIPS AND WATCHES THE FIRST HAND. SHE'LL SIT ON YUVAL'S LAP, OR SOMEONE ELSE'S. SHE DOESN'T PLAY, AND I DON'T THINK SHE HELPS ANYBODY EITHER. SHE'S VERY GOOD — SHE DOESN'T TELL ANYBODY WHO HAS WHAT CARDS."

KAREN'S ACADEMIC SPECIALTY IS MEDIEVAL SPANISH AND FRENCH LITERATURE, ESPECIALLY THE TRANSITION BETWEEN ORAL AND LITERATE TRADITIONS. "IN ORDER TO GET AT THAT, I LOOK AT THE EARLIEST BOOKS OF SONGS PUT TOGETHER BY MEDIEVAL AUTHORS. PAGE LAYOUT, ILLUSTRATIONS, AND SOUNDS — IT'S VERY DYNAMIC."

THALIA AND HER BALLERINA FRIEND.

SHE HAS LITTLE PATIENCE FOR FEMINIST THEORY, HOWEVER, OR FOR AMATEUR ANTHROPOLOGY. "I PROBABLY HAD TOO MUCH LITERARY THEORY SHOVED DOWN MY THROAT WHEN I WAS IN GRADUATE SCHOOL, SO I'M KIND OF RELUCTANT TO THEORIZE ABOUT GENDERED SPACES AND THINGS LIKE THAT," SHE SAYS. "ACADEMIA HAS MOVED ON NOW, THOUGH. NOW IT'S NOT FEMINISM, IT'S HOMOEROTICISM."

© 2002 GOLUS & WELCH

HOW aBouT a COWBOY POKeR NighT?

by Jake Austen

ONE OF THE MOST interesting aspects of poker is its association with the myths, legends, and truths about the Old West. So why not make your Thursday night game something special? How about recreating a historically accurate cowboy poker game in your very own home? Why should the Civil War recreationists have all the fun? Here are a few tips on how to make your cowboy poker night a yeehaw, yippy-ti-yi-yay, rootin' tootin' success.

1. **First things first: get some old-time cards.** You can't play cards without cards, can you? And you can't play cowboy poker with a newfangled deck. The main difference between a modern deck and a late-nineteenth-century deck (or as a cowpoke might say, a "California prayer book" or "railroad bible") is the numbers and letters (J, Q, K, and A) in the corners. Card buffs call these characters "indices," but cowboys likely wouldn't have used that phrase, especially because they didn't have any indices on their cards to talk about. Now it won't be easy to find new cards without numbers in the corners, but you could probably find an antique deck or a historically accurate facsimile on eBay. But is that really the cowboy way? Cowboys didn't have eBay. They had to make do with what they had and rely on their resourcefulness. So I suggest you take the

deck you have and either sand off the numbers or cover them up with white paint. It is true that the latter will make the cards heavier (especially if you use period-appropriate lead-based house paint). But that actually will be a bit more authentic. In olden days, cards were twice as heavy as today's because they consisted of the face of the card pasted to the back of the card (thus the other cowboy term "pasteboards"). Make sure you don't scuff or splatter paint on the backs of the cards, as the appearance of marked cards could lead to trouble (see tip number seven). I forgot to add that most cowboy-era decks also had what card collectors call "full-length single-ended court figures," meaning that the jacks, queens, and kings had legs (instead of existing as the bizarre, two-headed, conjoined-at-the-waist freaks we are used to today). This will be a little harder to alter, but Wyatt Earp would have figured out a way to deal with it, and you can, too!

2. Play poker the cowboy way. As popular as it is (and as Texan as it is) Texas hold 'em isn't the most authentic cowboy game (it emerged in the thirties or forties). If you wanna be a cowboy, you are going to have to stick to draw and stud poker, with jackpots (jacks or better to open). The history of poker in America sees the game gaining popularity in the 1830s and '40s, with the fifty-two-card deck becoming standard (as opposed to a twenty-card deck—just tens through aces). Fancy dudes on riverboats played draw poker, but the rough-and-tumble owlhoots preferred stud (they even played something called "horse stud"). Stud has more opportunity for bluffing and heavier play, so it was a better fit for cowboys who liked their recreation rough. Draw poker was certainly played in saloons—lots of legendary cowboy-poker-violence stories involve draw—but the more casual gambling (the equivalent of today's home games) was most likely limited to stud, even after the wild joker and all the variant games were introduced in the 1870s. So on your cowboy poker night, forgo rounds of spit in the ocean, anaconda, and

blind baseball. Few cowboys got to see the ocean, they saw more rat-
tlers than anacondas, and, though blindness was more prevalent in
those days than today, baseball was far less.

3. Dress the part. You can't get into the cowboy groove in penny
loafers and an Old Navy fleece pullover. You're gonna need to deck
yourself out in a cowboy hat, cowboy boots, and a cowboy shirt
(snaps instead of buttons). You can skip the chaps and spurs. Getting
your hands on some genuine buckaroo duds shouldn't be a problem
if you live in Texas or out West, where people actually still deal with
horses. If you are elsewhere, and live anywhere near a Mexican neighborhood, that's where you can usually find pretty amazing western-
wear shops (the cowpoke look has long been a fashion "do" in
Mexican menswear). If you live in, say, Bhopal, Djibouti, or Martha's
Vineyard, you may not have a Mexican neighborhood near your
home. But even if you have to buy your bolo tie by mail order or on-
line, it'll be OK as long as you remember one important rule: real-life
cowboys did not wear sequins or glitter. The cowboy from the Village People doesn't count. Nothing is more degrading to the cowboy
legacy than ornate, Vegas showgirl-style western wear. An easy rule
of thumb is that if the clothing would make it *more* difficult to wrestle a calf to the ground, then it is inappropriate. If you have to be
prissy, you can press a tight crease in your Wrangler jeans, à la country crooner George Strait—he's a genuine cowboy, so that's legit.

Another thing to remember when dressing up for historical recre-
ations: revisionism is OK if it makes everyone more comfortable.
When the White Sox play their "turn back the clock to 1917" game,
they still let the black players suit up, despite the historical inaccu-
racy. Thus, if everyone wants to be a cowboy, let everybody be a cowboy. If you're Chinese, there's no need to dress up as a railroad
laborer; if you're black, you don't have to wear a sharecropper getup;
and so forth. Let's just pretend we all got along, played cards
together, and shot each other (again, see number seven).

4. Drinks. There's a separate "poker drinks" chapter in this book
that contains some good suggestions for cowboy-theme swilling, but
it basically comes down to whiskey, whiskey, and more whiskey. If
you can't get those cool thick-bottomed "church window" glasses,
just go all out and have every player drink from the bottle. It actually may be a good idea to give each player his own bottle and forgo
sharing. Though sliding the bottle across the table may look cool in
the movies, nothing breaks the cowboy-poker mood like stopping to
clean the carpet with a roll of paper towels and a little seltzer.

Also, I know cowboys always order sarsaparilla in the movies, but
that's basically ginger ale. Don't be a wuss. Anyhow, nowadays with
all the crazy botanical, home-remedy action going on, it's easier to
buy raw, dirty sarsaparilla roots than it is to find a bottle of the pop.
Plus, it's reputed to have Viagra-esque effects on its imbibers, and
that's not really the best state to be in at the poker table.

5. Roll your own! Of course a smoky room is part of the game, but
to be an authentic cowpoke, avoid what the buckaroos called "pimp
sticks" (store-bought cigarettes). You need to get you some "makins"
(loose tobacco) and then "fill a blanket" (roll a cigarette). Here's a
quick how-to; but practice beforehand—you don't wanna look like
a greenhorn:

Fold the rolling paper long-ways if it ain't prefolded. Pour the
tabacky even-like in the fold. Push it 'round the paper to make sure
it's even all the way 'cross. Fold the paper top edge to bottom edge,
and begin rolling the makins back and forth 'til it's round and lightly
packed. Tuck the upper edge of the paper down, and start rollin'. For
this, you make a rolling motion with both of your thumbs and fore-
fingers. Give it a manly lick, and seal it up.

Now rolling cigarettes is easier to read about than do, but this
just might be a great opportunity for family bonding. After a brief
fall from grace in the 1980s, marijuana regained its status as the drug
of choice for high school kids throughout the '90s and across the

bridge into the new millennium. That means that if you have high-school-age kids, this could be the perfect chance to spend some quality time together by having them teach you proper rolling methods. If that option isn't available to you, a sexy alternative is renting the 1952 avant-garde western *Red Garters*, in which Marlene Dietrich teaches a fine-looking Rosemary Clooney to roll a cigarette.

6. One of the most important rules to remember if you play cowboy poker: Fold black aces and eights . . . quickly! This is known as the "dead man's hand." Legend has it that on August 2, 1876, James Butler Hickok (better known as scout, deputy marshal, and gunfighter Wild Bill Hickok) moseyed on into Nuttall & Mann's No. 10 Saloon in Deadwood, South Dakota. The poker table was rarin' to go, and Carl Mann, the saloon's owner, Captain W. R. Massic, a riverboat pilot, and Charles Rich, a gunman and gambling buddy of Wild Bill, were already seated. As a rule, Wild Bill never sat with his back to the door, but after negotiations to switch seats with supposed-friend Rich failed, Hickok took the only open chair. As the game got underway, Jack McCall, a drifter, barfly, and ne'er-do-well, stealthly entered the room, positioned himself three feet from Hickok, and then (to quote Deadwood's only newspaper, *The Black Hills Pioneer*), "raised his revolver, and exclaiming, 'damn you, take that,' fired; the ball entering at the back of the head, and coming out at the center of the right cheek causing instant death." It is believed McCall shot Hickok to enhance his own reputation, though at the time he claimed the act was to avenge his brother's death (he was acquitted on that defense before being retried on a technicality and hanged). For the most part, the information above seems pretty credible and well documented. The legend part comes in when we learn that after being shot Hickok slumped over, revealing that he was holding black aces and black eights. This hand has forever gone down in poker lore as the "dead man's hand." (He also held the jack of diamonds, for you detail buffs.) OK, in retrospect, the lesson here isn't to fold that hand; it's actually not to sit with your back to the door. But cowpokes are a superstitious lot.

7. Pack a pistol. Apparently a lot of old-time cowboy poker ended in gunplay. In addition to Mr. Hickok's death (an anomaly; Wild Bill wasn't killed by a fellow player), Old West lore is smothered with tales of trigger turmoil at the tables. After slowly killing many a dental patient by coughing tuberculosis germs down their throats, John H. "Doc" Holliday shot poker rivals in Dallas (with a Colt .36); Jacksborough, Texas (with a .31 caliber pocket revolver); and Trinidad, Colorado (with a Remington .41 RF double derringer). He also shot fellow gamesters in Ft. Griffin, Texas, Las Vegas, Sante Fe, and Tombstone. He merely stabbed a dude to death in Denver (they had a no-guns-in-town rule).

John Wesley Hardin, a minister's son, was perhaps the deadliest gunman in the Old West, killing at least forty-four people during his vicious nine-year spree. On Christmas Day, 1869, Santa smiled on sixteen-year-old Hardin, who found himself $1,000 ahead in a no-limit poker game in Towash-on-the-Brazos, Texas. Unfortunately, "Big" Bradley, who ran the town, got a lump of coal in his stocking. The big loser in the game, he compounded his losses by drawing his gun on Hardin, who then shot him in the heart and head with a .45.

Even the ladies got in on the action. "Poker Alice" Duffield, a well-heeled English attorney's daughter, not only excelled at Old West card tables, but also proved adept with her Starr Army .44, shooting a man who accused her husband of cheating at cards. (A brilliant card counter, she was rarely challenged as a cheater herself.)

The lesson learned from all of this is simple: it doesn't matter what kind of gun you use; just make sure you kill somebody!

8. Bone up on your lingo. Here are some Old West phrases and slang that might come up if your night is going well: "got the bulge" (have the advantage); "shavetail" (an inexperienced person); "tenderfoot" (another inexperienced person); "buffalo" (to bluff); "eucher" (to outsmart someone); "hunky dorey" (good); "fandango" (a big party); "greenbacks" (money); "Lincoln skins" (more money); "high, low, jack, and the game" (successfully accomplished task).

A less successful night at the table may require the following glossary: "mudsill" (disreputable person); "gig" (cheat); "sold his saddle" (broke); "knock galley west" (beat senseless); "heeled" (armed with a gun); "Arkansas toothpick" (a large knife); "goner" (dead); "hoosegow" (jail); "tarnation" (eternal damnation).

9. Rent a bunch of westerns. There were hundreds of classic westerns released between the 1910s and the early 1950s, and a good number of them contain poker scenes. Just because these films were low-budget, assembly-line, semi-scripted knockoffs that often were shot in one day, it doesn't mean they weren't historically accurate. Then again, if these are true-to-life tales, then the majority of real-estate deals in the Old West involved deeds passing from innocent rubes to ruthless cheats in crooked card games. Even if the history is a bit convoluted, considering that the actors were only a generation or two removed from real cowboy days, I'm sure there's some accuracy to their card table decorum. Pay these tumbleweed thespians the honor of emulating their gambling style. A few titles with interesting poker-game scenes: *The Girl of the Golden West* (1915), *Rounding Up the Law* (1922), *Iron Rider* (1926), *Aces and Eights* (1932—opens with a lesson in luck, illustrated by he-of-the-unlucky-hand, Wild Bill Hickok), *The Riding Tornado* (1932), *Fargo Express* (1933), *The Roaring West* (1935), *The Desert Trail* (1935—John Wayne!), *Three Godfathers* (1936—Walter Brennan helps a total stranger cheat at poker for no real reason, explaining, "I guess I'm just a no-good rat"), *Song of the Trail* (1936), *Aces Wild* (1937), *Black Aces* (1937), *Six Gun Trail* (1938), *Destry Rides Again* (1939), *Oklahoma Kid* (1939—gangsters ride the range . . . Cagney and Bogie in a western!), *Sunset Trail* (1939), *The Carson City Kid* (1940), *West* *of Pinto Basin* (1940), *Kid's Last Ride* (1941), *Dudes are Pretty People* (1942—not a gay porno; actually, a title in a series of Hal Roach comic westerns), *Raiders of the Range* (1942), *Tall in the Saddle* (1944—contains some excellent cowboy-poker advice: whatever you do, don't try to cheat John Wayne!), *Wells Fargo Days* (1944), *Gentleman from Texas* (1946), *Loaded Pistols* (1948—Gene Autry literally pulls his buddy's gun out of the kitty. Another good cowboy poker rule: don't put your pistol in the pot.).

10. **Be careful!** Make sure you don't commit to a game of cowboy poker at a rodeo. That particular event involves four "cowboys" playing poker at a card table in the middle of the arena. A bull is then released, and the beast makes a beeline for the action. Last cowboy in his chair wins the pot. Actually, if you are a particularly poor player, this may be your best chance to come out a winner.

FiFty-twO HOuse rules

H ERE'S A COLLECTION of etiquette guidelines, traditions, and
nonstandard rules (some archaic, some absurd, and some con-
founding) that add flavor to home games around the world. Bringing some of these to your neighborhood showdown may make for
some interesting nights. But be warned: bring any of these into a
casino, and others will see your head as a giant Warner Brothers cartoon lollipop (you sucker)!

1. Acey-deucey. A side bet that a third card in succession will fall in
rank between the first two.

2. Around-the-corner straight. A house rule that is scoffed at in
every serious poker game in the world. It allows for a straight that
uses the ace as both higher than a king and lower than a two (thus
Q-K-A-2-3 would be a straight). Some games specify that this ranks
just below a real straight, but above three of a kind. At others, this
is higher than a real straight and lower than a flush.

3. Beer fine. At the end of the night, whoever brought the six-pack
that has the most bottles (or cans) left in it has to cover everyone's
last ante. This either prevents people from bringing cheap or off-

brand beer, or it encourages the person who brought the bad beer to drink it himself.

4. Big bobtail. In a five-card game, a four-card straight flush (beats a flush, but not four of a kind).

5. Big cat. An archaic ranking hand. A big cat (also called a big tiger) is five cards, all between eight and king, with no pairs and no straight. Ranks above a little cat and below a flush.

6. Big dog. An archaic ranking hand. A big dog is five cards, all between nine and ace, with no pairs and no straight. Ranks above a little dog and below a little cat.

7. Black Maria. "Black Maria" is a nickname for the queen of spades, and there are several different games by that name in which she has certain powers if drawn. The Black Maria house rule (applicable to any game in which the dealer invokes it) is that if one of your up cards is the queen of spades, you have to throw $5 into the pot.

8. Black power. In five-card stud, an all-black hand (mixed spades and clubs) beats high card, but is lower than a pair.

9. Blaze. All face cards. This hand ranks higher than a flush and lower than a full house.

10. Bobtail flush. In a five-card game, four cards of the same suit. This ranks higher than a pair, but lower than two pair.

11. Bug. A joker can only be used as an ace or to fill a flush or straight.

12. Cell phones off!

13. Cigar rule. The big winner is responsible to bring cigars to the next game.

14. Democracy/seniority. If something unusual comes up, and no rule books cover it, consensus by everyone at the table not involved in the dispute rules. If that doesn't work (say, if everyone is involved in the dispute), the senior player at the table (the oldest player or the player who has been in the game the longest) decides.

15. Dutch straight. An obscure ranking hand that is made up of sequential odd or even number and face cards (2-4-6-8-10 or 5-7-9-J-K, for example). Ranks above three of a kind and below a straight.

16. Elvis has left the building. The first player to leave the game has to cover everyone's ante for the next hand.

17. Fines. Fines (paid to the pot, they're usually just an extra ante, but may be more if deemed necessary) are levied for misdeals, flashing cards, splashing the pot, or just saying or doing something really stupid. The table determines the fine, and any protest results in another fine.

18. Five of a kind. Some home games that use wild cards refuse to accept that such a hand as five of a kind exists. When it is recognized, it is said to be higher than a straight flush.

19. Free hand. In a rotating dealer's choice game, the dealer has an option to deal a quick hand of five card stud before declaring the more elaborate game he wants to play.

20. High spade. A side bet in draw poker. Whoever has the highest spade wins.

21. House change. When cashing in chips at the end of the night, anyone with a remainder of chips of less than a dollar donates those chips to the host's pile.

22. Indian. This goes by many names (it is sometimes called "idiot" or "fool's poker"), and it involves each player betting on a card that is stuck to his forehead facing outward. Everyone bets with knowledge of all cards but his own. This game is often played as a last hand of the night.

23. Last bet. The betting in a round begins with the player who initiated the betting on the previous round (if there was no raise), or with the player who put in the last raise that was called in the previous round (rank of cards on table don't determine the first bet).

24. Late report. The tardiest member (usually the same guy every week) is responsible for providing the score of the in-progress baseball or basketball game at the time he parked. If he does not have that information, he is required to return to his car and get it. (TVs and radios are banned during game play.)

25. Lazy Edna. A high-low game in which each player only gets one card, face down, followed by one round of betting.

26. Leaving the table. If you have to leave the table mid-hand, you forfeit your claim to the pot, and no empty chair will be dealt to, even if you only have to leave for a second.

27. Lightweight. If you go light, and then win the pot, you have to pay 10 percent interest (on whatever amount you went light) to the next kitty. (If you lose the hand, you just settle up at face value.)

28. Little cat. An archaic ranking hand. A little cat is five cards, all between three and nine, with no pairs and no straight. Ranks above a big dog and below a big cat.

29. Little dog. An archaic ranking hand. A little dog is five cards, all between two and seven, with no pairs and no straight. Ranks above a straight and below a big dog.

30. Mandatory side bet. The dealer is required to make a mandatory side bet with the player on his right (the bet could be about anything; creativity is encouraged). The loser throws a dollar into the pizza-and-beer fund. If you play sixty hands with six players, you have the potential of throwing $10 in the pot, but you could also win every side bet and get your food and drink free.

31. No check-raise. The banning of check-raising, a controversial rule in home games, dictates that if a player checks, he is not allowed to raise in the same round. Many home games swear by this rule to offset the deceptive nature of checking to see what everyone else will do even though the player who check-raises plans on betting. Poker purists argue that deception is the heart of the game.

32. No couples. Husbands and wives, girlfriends and boyfriends, and domestic partners cannot play in the same game, as their intertwined fortunes leave too much possibility for collusion.

33. Pass etiquette. No one is supposed to pick up his or her cards in a game that involves passing (such as anaconda and its variants) until all players have passed their cards.

34. Potting out. A mutual agreement to take money out of a pot to buy food, drinks, cigars, or cigarettes.

35. Poverty. If a player loses his money he is allowed to keep playing, usually with some kind of caveat (such as returning his free buy-in to its source if he ends up winning, be it to the pot, the collective players, or to an individual player. Some tables have the player donate any winnings to the last pot.). If the player keeps losing, he or she is eventually out.

36. Scrabble challenge. If a player insists on a disputed rule and the rule book proves him wrong, the player is fined an extra dollar's ante into the next pot. This is so named because in Scrabble, players are punished for losing a dictionary challenge. In the future, this may be renamed the NFL instant replay challenge.

37. Second table. If a big crowd shows up, necessitating a second table, cards are drawn. The half with the low cards goes to the second, new, table and the half with the high cards stays at the regular table.

38. Secret woman-defense rule. When a men's table is joined by a superior woman player, regulars make sure elaborate wild card games are called so that when they lose to her, they can blame it on "girl's rules."

39. Seven shuffles. A deck must be riffle-shuffled seven times before it can be dealt. This is based on a 1986 study, published in *American Mathematical Monthly*, about the sufficient number of shuffles required to achieve an acceptable degree of disorder in a deck of fifty-two cards.

40. Seven up. In seven-card stud, any sevens that are up are wild. No cards in the hole are wild. Not to be confused with a more elaborate game of the same name.

41. Skeet. An obscure ranking hand in five-card draw containing a two, five, and nine with one card falling in rank between the two and the five and the last card between the five and the nine. A very confusing rule. This ranks above three of a kind and below a straight.

42. Stud marker. A marker, such as a pocket knife, is thrown into the first pot. The winner of that pot must deal stud when it is his turn to deal. The knife is placed back into the pot when the player who has won the knife deals. This means that, on average, you will play two hands of stud per round, and draw poker the rest of the time.

43. Suicide kings. In addition to the standard king of hearts (considered the "suicide king" because he has buried a broadsword nearly to the hilt in his left temple), the king of diamonds is also considered to be taking his life, because he is about to split the back of his skull open with a battle axe.

44. Suit ranks. Many home games, as a backup to avoid ties, have a ranking of suits. Though the rankings vary, I have usually experienced it as, from highest to lowest, spades, hearts, clubs, diamonds (perhaps this is a variation of the suit rankings in bridge, in which diamonds rank higher than clubs). In Europe, I'm told, it goes hearts, diamonds, clubs, spades (they value the heart more over there). If you play suit ranks, just make sure that everyone agrees on the ranking before the cards are dealt.

45. Table washer. First one to lose his or her original buy-in has to wash the drink glasses before being allowed another buy-in.

46. Toking. Tipping the dealer for dealing you a winner.

47. Twist. In a five-card high-low game, the option to replace any of your cards after all five have been dealt. There is an additional round of betting after the twist cards are dealt.

48. The two-minute rule. Players have only two minutes to do something with their hands when play comes around to them. If they break the rule, they forfeit their claim to the pot and are automatically out of the hand. This rule is usually invoked as a threat to a slow player rather than enacted as a punishment.

49. Wangdoodle. A round in which the ante or maximum raise is drastically increased. Sometimes played last hand of the night, other times after an amazing hand loses.

50. Winner antes. After winning a healthy pot, the victor picks up antes for the table.

51. Winners wash. Winners clean up after the game.

52. Wrong cards. If someone picks up cards meant for another player, the player whose cards they should have been has the option of being a good sport and taking the remaining cards on the table or taking the cards intended for him while the other player has to sit out the hand.

Fifty-two Poker Terms

Part of what makes poker night fun is acting like a bunch of knowledgeable low-life big shots (of course, real low-life big shots have poker nights, too; they don't have to pretend). In order to play this role, one needs to sling some poker lingo. Nothing makes you feel more authentic than fluency in the foreign language that is Poker Talk. Here are a few fun phrases to use with your buddies (don't try some of these in the casino!), culled from common poker slang, outdated old-time lingo, and creative neighborhood games from across the country. Use 'em early and often.

1. Nut hand (or "the nuts"). The best possible hand in any given game; unbeatable cards. This is the perfect poker term because it is vulgar, it is relevant to the game, and it is just fun to say. I prefer the singular, as it doubles the vulgarity; "nut" can refer to both a testicle and ejaculate. This versatility makes derivations (second nut, low nut, etc.) even filthier.

2. Rags. Worthless cards that don't help your hand.

3. Dog table. The second, inferior table (named after the dogs-playing-poker paintings). Whenever a home game is big enough that it has to split into two groups, this is what you call the less appealing table (the one without women players, the one without fun personalities, etc.).

4. Belly buster. The card you need to make an inside straight.

5. Bullwhip effect. Experienced by the chump caught in the middle when the high and low eventual winners keep raising.

6. Souping. Raising in stud before the first turn because everyone else has shitty cards showing. All you're trying to do is win the antes, which in the old days was just enough to buy some soup.

7. Splash (or "splash the pot"). To throw, instead of place, one's chips into the pot. This isn't cool, because it's a common way to cheat by shorting the pot.

8. Being snackface. Failure to provide adequate/acceptable snacks when hosting a game.

9. Steel wheel. A five-high straight. This is more commonly shortened to simply "the wheel," likely out of the shame of your winning hand being associated with the Rolling Stones's weak 1989 *Steel Wheels* album and tour.

10. Muck. The pile of folded cards. Crafty cheaters try to eye good cards in the muck and then stack the deck.

11. On tilt. A player who is pissed off or annoyed and is consequently playing worse. It is an unfriendly strategy to get someone intentionally on tilt to improve your own winnings.

12. High beta. The big winner or loser.

13. Crimping. Sweating even though you're not hot. When you get this nervous in the game, maybe it's time to consider going home.

14. Uglies (as in "ugly Americans"). Guest players who insist that rules and procedures should conform to the way they do them in their usual home game. "Who invited the ugly?"

15. Down and dirty. Something to announce with sinister glee when you get your last card in seven-card stud (even though all seventh cards are dealt down, no matter their cleanliness).

16. Make a cow. To split a pot.

17. Sleeper. A stray chip. Some players will compulsively steal even your lowly nickel chip if it strays too far from your pile—watch out!

18. Zombie. An amazingly poker-faced player, or a very poor choice of drinks for poker night.

19. Folder's paradise. A game where the dealer is the only one who antes. So called because it encourages conservative players to fold without losing anything.

20. Blivit. A shitty hand with nothing in it.

21. Going piggy (or "going oinky," or "shooting the moon"). Going both ways in a high/low game.

22. Undressed. You get "undressed" if the cards you need show up on the table in someone else's hand. If you're showing two aces early in stud and the other aces are showing elsewhere by the time all the cards are dealt, you got undressed.

23. Kibitzer. A nonplayer who just hangs out around the game, annoying people (or possibly cheating with a partner).

24. Mexican standoff. A split pot on a tie.

25. Rainbow. Three or four cards of different suits in a hand or in a flop.

26. Dead man's hand. Black aces and black eights. Wild Bill Hickok was allegedly shot while holding this hand.

27. Rockets. Aces. This is most often used when you have two aces in the hole ("pocket rockets").

28. Death card. The ace of spades (not because Hickok was holding one in his "dead man's hand," or because Motörhead's song "Ace of Spades" influenced death metal, but because of its symbolic meaning in tarot-card fortune telling).

29. Puppy foot. The ace of clubs.

30. Deuces. Twos.

31. Crabs. Threes, because a three supposedly looks like a crab with pinchers.

32. Sailboats. Fours, because they sort of look like sailboats.

33. Sinks. Fives (as in *cinco* or *cinque*).

34. Washington Monument. Three fives (the Washington Monument is 555 feet tall).

35. **Satans.** Sixes.

36. **Iron Maiden.** Three sixes (an homage to British heavy metal band Iron Maiden's hit song, "Number of the Beast").

37. **Luckys.** Sevens

38. **Snowmen.** Eights, for those of you so lazy that you make your snowmen with only two sections.

39. **No-no's.** Nines (from the German *nein*).

40. **Bo Dereks.** Tens.

41. **Judge Bean.** Three tens (Bean was famous for handing out thirty-day sentences).

42. **Johnnys.** Jacks.

43. **Bitches.** Queens.

44. **Hookers.** Queens.

45. ***Putas.*** Queens (Spanish for hooker, the previous three aren't that genteel . . . maybe you could also just say "ladies" or "broads").

46. **Siegfried and Roy.** A pair of queens.

47. **Six tits.** Three queens.

48. **Village People.** Four queens (though there were actually five Village People, so I'm assuming this phrase is either used incorrectly, or

with the knowledge that Victor Willis, the original cop, wasn't actually gay).

49. Cowboys. Kings.

50. Shaka Zulus. Black kings (source: *The Bernie Mac Show*).

51. Alabama night riders. Three kings (KKK, as in Ku Klux Klan— not the most pleasant image for your poker table).

52. Ice Cube, George Clooney, and Marky Mark. Three kings (now there's a prettier image).

◆ *A Waterloo by C.M. Coolidge* ◆

POKER IN CULTURE

It's a Dog's World, According to Coolidge

by Moira F. Harris

BROWN & BIGELOW, a St. Paul printing company, opened its doors for business in 1896. In this new firm, Horace Brown, a printer, joined Herbert Bigelow, a salesman, to enter the relatively new field of "remembrance advertising," a concept that promoted imprinted objects a business could give to its customers in thanks for their patronage. Over time, the most famous Brown & Bigelow product became the calendar, but later lines also included playing cards, desk blotters, and various forms of leather gifts.

Brown & Bigelow did not invent the calendar as an advertising idea. Over the years, however, the company has become known as one of the nation's leading printers and publishers of this form of art and advertising. For its calendars, B & B hired some of the best-known American illustrators to paint either a single image or a series. Charles Russell, Norman Rockwell, and Maxfield Parrish are among the artists who worked with B & B. Rockwell's series of Boy Scout images, Lawson Smith's comic monkeys, Rolf Armstrong's pinup girls, and Andrew Loomis's happy scenes of the Dionne quintuplets were longtime B & B bestsellers.

One artist whose distinctive calendars are well known, but whose identity is not, is Cassius Marcellus Coolidge (1844–1934). If you asked an antiques dealer or the proprietor of a stand at a flea market if he had any calendars by Coolidge for sale, the answer would be "no." Ask again for calendars with poker-playing dogs on them and the light dawns. Coolidge's dogs played poker, went to ball games, camped in the woods, and danced elegantly at New Year's Eve parties. Eyeglasses perched on their broad noses, fat cigars in their mouths, Coolidge's dogs sat around tables covered with cards, poker chips, ashtrays, and shot glasses. It was clearly a male dog's world, which a female dog entered only by permission.

While commercial artists whose work is created for hire are not always well known, B & B identified its artists in annual brochures sent to customers. Many of the artists signed their work, yet Coolidge, despite his success, remains relatively anonymous. He deserves more attention for his achievements, which have spun their way from calendars to imitations in murals and truck paintings created far from Minnesota and Coolidge's home state of New York.

C. M. Coolidge was born in Philadelphia, New York, in 1844. As a young man he moved to the nearby town of Antwerp, where he became a partner in a drugstore in 1868. He founded *The Antwerp News* in 1871, and the town's first bank a year later. In addition, he painted street signs and numbered the town's houses. After a trip to Europe, he moved to Rochester in 1873. There he opened another drugstore and became interested in photography. He is credited with the invention of "photographic caricatures," humorous drawings of headless bodies on cardboard (the patron stood behind the body, adding his face to the composition). By the early 1880s, he had moved once more, to New York City.

Coolidge is said to have done artwork for cigar companies, which used his paintings for lithographed box covers or inner box lids. Known Coolidge art includes a drawing of a wide-eyed child, called *Injured Innocence*, which appeared in *Harper's Weekly* in February 1878, and a poster for the Columbia Bicycle Company of Massachusetts, which shows a parrot and a monkey riding a bicycle. He was well known as a painter of dogs prior to his affiliation with Brown & Bigelow, but it is his calendar art that lives on.

Coolidge signed his first contract with Brown & Bigelow in 1906. At that time the company's calendars were usually printed with one tip-in illustration and a small pad of twelve sheets serving as the calendar. As one commentator noted, a calendar with one humorous illustration could become very trite as it hung on the wall over a twelve-month span. A calendar with twelve illustrations to be flipped over or torn off was the logical innovation in printing.

Between 1906 and his death in 1934, Coolidge painted sixteen paintings of dogs for Brown & Bigelow. The company used them for the calendars, playing cards, postcards, and blotters that it manufactured. The designs were licensed to other companies, which published prints of the Coolidge dog paintings as sets. Prints of the poker-playing dogs, often in a series of five or six images, were sold as recently as the 1970s for $3 per set. Antique dealers now charge $10 to $30 per picture, framed or unframed.

Brown & Bigelow no longer owns the original Coolidge dog paintings. Once photographs were made of them, the original paintings were sold through the company store or otherwise dispersed into private collections. For the past twenty years, Coolidge paintings have been offered for sale through various auction houses in New York and Washington, D.C. Prices have ranged from $1,000 to as high as $74,000 per painting.

No humans appear in the sixteen dog paintings Coolidge sold to B & B, but the male, middle-class lifestyle is clearly there. For his poker-playing crowd, Coolidge preferred large dogs: collies, mastiffs, Great Danes, and St. Bernards, who sit comfortably in leather chairs pulled up around a card table. On the dark walls of their den or clubroom hang thick curtains and dark paintings; the only light is the artificial gleam of a lamp hanging over the table. Once Coolidge had established his cast of characters, he gave them additional exposure by painting the scene again with minor changes. The same five dogs appear in B & B's *A Bold Bluff* and *A Waterloo*, as well as in an untitled work from a private collection shown in Carla Davidson's 1973 article for *American Heritage*. These three paintings tell a story. In the untitled work the game has begun. The St. Bernard holds a pipe, while the serving wench (a poodle with a bow in her hair) brings a trayful of drinks. In *A Bold Bluff*, the St. Bernard has switched from his pipe to a cigar, and the pile of chips in the center of the table has grown larger. The St. Bernard stops smoking entirely in *A Waterloo*, as he needs both paws to rake in all his winnings. The four other dogs, calm in the first painting, apprehensive in the second, bark with outrage in painting three as they see the St. Bernard's cards face up.

Another pair of related paintings is B & B's *Poker Sympathy* and *The Poker Game* (offered in an Adam Weschler auction on October 3, 1992). In each painting, seven dogs confront an eighth dog across a card table. Cards fall through the air and a drink is spilled as an angry bulldog climbs on the table to accuse the culprit, who slides lower in his chair while gazing with the fear of the guilty toward the

◆ *A Bold Bluff* ◆

◆ *His Station and Four Aces* ◆

viewer. Coolidge changes some elements (such as the breed of the accused), but the two paintings essentially delineate the same tale.

Confrontation is the main element in three other poker scenes Coolidge painted for B & B. In *Sitting up with a Sick Friend*, two hat-wearing female terriers break up the male dogs' game. In *Pinched with Four Aces*, four dogs in police uniforms halt another card game, while in *His Station and Four Aces*, the dog–train conductor comes to inform a suit-wearing St. Bernard that the train is nearing his stop and that he may have to disembark before playing his winning hand with its four aces.

Coolidge's poker-playing dogs, partying at home or on the train, formed an obvious series. These paintings were printed as thousands of lithographs by B & B. With a few slight changes, the same scenes were painted more than once by Coolidge. Although the artist painted other scenes of dogs dressed in human garb and involved in human activities, it was the poker-playing dogs that became his specialty.

Information is not available on the exact years that Coolidge submitted paintings to Brown & Bigelow once he had signed a contract.

The February 1909 issue of the company's magazine, *The Business Builder*, notes that Coolidge had already submitted both *A Bold Bluff* and *A Waterloo*. For the B & B 1910 calendars, the new Coolidge paintings were *Breach of Promise Suit* and *Dog of a Bachelor*, a study of a single collie.

In *Breach of Promise Suit, New Year's Eve in Dogville, Riding the Goat*, and *One to Tie and Two to Win*, Coolidge attempted scenes filled with activity. A court case, a tea dance, a circus act performed for a royal couple, and a baseball game gave the artist the opportunity to enlarge his settings and expand his roster of canine characters. It would seem, however, that B & B felt that their customers preferred fewer dogs and indoor locations where both alcohol and tobacco were part of the ambiance. Nine of the sixteen Coolidge paintings show dogs with cards, poker chips, cigars, or, as in *The Reunion*, a bottle of whisky and a meerschaum pipe for each collie. For Coolidge, an artist who had earlier sold his paintings to cigar companies, it was natural to give his dogs something to smoke.

Where did Coolidge get the idea for his poker-playing caricatures of dogs? That may never be known, but certainly the idea of humanized dogs was not unusual in nineteenth-century art, either at the Royal Academy level or in more popular forms of culture such as postcards, magazine illustrations, ceramic figures, children's books, or sheet-music covers. Advertisers have long found that either fierce or cuddly canines, clothed or not, are appealing logos or symbols for their products. That tradition extends easily from RCA Victor's Nipper to Sun Microsystems' late-'90s Bernese mountain dog, Network.

Dogs have long been depicted in art, in scenes of hunting and warfare or as emblems of loyalty and devotion. By the early 1800s, artists, especially those in England, were being commissioned by pet owners to paint portraits of the family whippet, Newfoundland, or setter. The English painter Sir Edwin Landseer is credited with having transformed the study of these pedigreed and cherished pets into anecdotal genre scenes where the canine characters revealed their emotional ties to the human members of the households. Landseer's dogs already had human sensibilities. It was an easy step to give dogs (or cats, pigs, bears, and rabbits) human attributes and clothing as well.

Copies, imitations, and parodies are a sign of a successful artist's fame and continued influence. During his lifetime Grant Wood could combat the misuse of his *American Gothic* couple, but now that pair is as frequently parodied as da Vinci's *Mona Lisa* and Edvard Munch's *The Scream*. The success of Coolidge's dogs led to similar imitations and parodies. A Minnesota artist, Bryan Moon, produces lithographs of hat-and-gun wearing dogs standing lineup style as the Magnificent Seven or the Hunt Club. In another reference to Coolidge's specialty, an ad in a magazine for llama raisers featured a group portrait, in pastels, of elegantly dressed llamas seated around a poker table. According to the advertiser, they were planning an auction in Reno, so poker-playing llamas seemed most appropriate. When *Wired* magazine wanted to suggest that Microsoft's Bill Gates was "playing with the big boys," the magazine (April 1998) featured an illustration of Gates at a poker table with Coolidge-type dogs.

For an unknown artist in Juarez, the dogs' game was not poker but billiards. His painting of a poolroom filled with canine players appeared on black velvet. In a recent book about paintings on velvet, the author noted Coolidge's influence on the genre, although the immediate source was probably (fellow anthropomorphic gambling-dog artist) Arthur Sarnoff's *The Hustler*. A lithograph of this same scene made its way to Iraq, where it was offered for sale, in a heavy gilt frame, at a Baghdad flea market, according to a photograph in the *New York Times*. With subtle variations, both poker- and pool-playing dogs were painted on the back doors of Colombian *chivás* (trucks) by a painter nicknamed Tarzan, and by a Panamanian artist on a city bus.

Coolidge-descended dogs appear once more in two murals, painted on a Redwood City, California, pool hall. On one, a local artist named Flavio has painted the same breeds, but with an addition.

A female poodle dressed in frilly blouse and skirt brandishes her umbrella as she drags home her mastiff spouse, just as Coolidge's lady dogs did in *Sitting up with a Sick Friend*.

The second mural on the Club San Luis's windows shows the last scene of Coolidge's poker game. A hound gathers up the pot (now in bills rather than chips) while the other players gaze sadly or leave while pulling out empty pockets. The scene is not Coolidge's elegant den, but a cheaply paneled room with a calendar (not an oil painting) hanging on the wall. These dogs wear vests and pants with suspenders, suggesting working-class players rather than Coolidge's businessmen.

To some critics, Coolidge's poker-playing dogs are banal images, stereotypes, kitsch at its worst. To others, they are amusing commentaries on human nature. To advertisers, they are appropriate images to sell products ranging from cigars and beer to gasoline engines and cyclone fences. Despite Coolidge's anonymity, his dogs have not lost their popularity. Recent catalogs offered lithographs of *A Friend in Need*, and shirts and a necktie showing its central action: the exchange, paw to paw, of an ace between two bulldogs. One episode of the long-running television sitcom *Cheers* involved an argument between Sam and Diane about taste in art. He was proud of his framed reproduction of the poker-playing dogs, which she detested.

Perhaps the most appropriate evocation of the lasting fame of Coolidge's specialty was in a television commercial produced for a Minnesota State Lottery game called "Showdown Poker." Three men enter a museum gallery, exclaiming to each other over the quality of its art. As the camera brings one painting into view, these appreciative aesthetes happily admire Coolidge's perennial gamblers, his poker-playing dogs. For the ad agency, it was the perfect image, since it stressed neither instant wealth nor gambling. It referred, instead, to the fun of the game, using players everyone would recognize.

POKER IN THE MOVIES

We asked some of our favorite filmmakers, film critics, and just plain film fans to tell us their favorite poker moments in the movies. Skipping the coming attractions and getting right to the feature, here is what they had to say.

Austin Vince (experimental filmmaker). The best poker scene *ever* was in *For a Few Dollars More* (1965). Clint Eastwood, in the role of Monco, arrives in the small town of White Rocks on the trail of wanted outlaw Red "Baby" Cavanagh. Monco arrives in the saloon where Red is playing poker, interrupts the game, and slowly deals a hand to each player. Cards are exchanged and Red lays down his hand: three kings, a ten, and a queen. Monco slowly and deliberately flicks his hand down on top of Red's; it's three aces, a queen, and a jack. Red glances up at Monco and casually asks: "I didn't hear what that bet was?" Monco responds: "Your life." Red reaches for his pistol, but Monco chops him down with a mighty karate blow! The ensuing punch-up sees Monco sparring with only his left hand, the right kept under his poncho throughout. With Red knocked senseless, Monco beseeches him: "Alive or dead, it's your choice."

Rachel Lichtman (comedian). In *Goodfellas* (1990), the guys are playing cards, just kinda bullshitting around the table, when Spider (Michael Imperioli, who played Christopher in *The Sopranos*), who's kinda slow, fucks up the drink order. So Tommy (Joe Pesci) starts to fuck with him. He pulls out his gun, and he's like, "dance, motherfucker, dance," you know, that kinda thing. And then he actually shoots Spider in the foot! *And then they go back to playing cards!* So later Spider works up the balls to tell Joe Pesci to go fuck himself, and everyone (but Pesci) laughs. So Pesci gets pissed off and shoots Spider dead. Then around the table it's like, "Aw c'mon . . . *you're digging the hole,*" that kinda talk, and they stop playing. So that actually ends a goodfellas poker game. But shooting someone in the foot does not!

Nolan Dalla (professional gambler/writer). Even with its flawed ending, *The Cincinnati Kid* (1966) is the best poker movie of all time. It was the first film ever to show that cardplaying is a skill and can be a respectable profession. The movie's best poker scene does not even involve a poker hand. It's a thirty-second film clip of Steve McQueen sitting in a chair alone in a hallway, preparing himself for the big game with villain Edward G. Robinson. McQueen is about to play the game of his life—and he knows it. He pulls out a probability chart and begins slowly poring over the data, memorizing the percentages, trying to fine-tune himself in order to gain every conceivable edge in the game. This is what serious poker playing involves. It's not about fancy cars, flashy clothes, or the images normally associated with successful gambling. It shows that in poker, as in life, hard work and mastery of craft are normally the prerequisites for winning.

Derek Emerson (documentary filmmaker). *Cotton Candy* (1982), starring Clint Howard (who cowrote it with his brother, the film's director, and future Oscar winner, Ron Howard) is an *awesome,* funny movie. It's about teenagers forming a band (called Cotton Candy) and Battle of the Band–ing it out against rival group Rapid Fire (who repeatedly play a horrendous version of "I Shot the Sheriff" throughout the movie). Midway through the flick they have a band practice that goes sour due to a power failure. To pass the time, the guys (and their foxy female drummer) decide to play a game of strip poker. Just at the point when the drummer loses the game and has to get naked, the band leader (Charles Martin Smith, who was also in *American Graffiti*) steps in and puts the kibosh on, explaining that seeing her naked would change the band dynamic and could break them up. Judging by the horny looks on the other bandmates faces, they were more than willing to take that chance. Damn you, Charles! This scene underscores the innocence that makes this film what it is—cheesy but brilliant!

Rudy Ray Moore (actor). I did a film in Taipei, China, called *Big Willie from North Philly*—that was three years ago, it never came out. It was a gambling poker game all the way through the film, and I kicked asses and talked about them and had all the money on the table when the game was over. It was me, Jimmy Lynch, a Chinese girl, the baron of the casino, and some others around the table. We had thousands and thousands of dollars worth of fake money, money that looked like real money, in hundred-dollar bills. And I remember one of the men that I beat so badly, he fell out and died on top of the money, and I just kept playing, beating the rest of them with him dead on the table. It was a nice film, but it never came out.

Todd Alley (freelance writer). I know my already-suspect masculinity will be called further into question on this one, but I'd have to say my favorite cinematic poker scene takes place in *Mr. Mom* (1983). Michael Keaton going toe-to-toe with a table full of housewives in a high-stakes game of clip 'n' save–coupon poker. . . . Kenny Rogers can't touch that.

Kenyatta Sullivan (tavern owner). My favorite movie poker moment has always been from David Mamet's *House Of Games* (1987). A female psychiatrist (Lindsay Crouse) has gone to a gambling den in order to try and clear a debt one of her patients has run up with the local toughs, led by Mike (Joe Mantegna). Mike agrees to cancel the debt if she'll sit in on a high-stakes poker game in the backroom with him, pretending to be his girlfriend, watching for "tells." A tell is when a card player unconsciously tells his opponents how strong his hand is with his posture, or a nervous tic. In this case, she's watching for one guy in particular to nervously twist his ring (played by Ricky Jay, a notorious old-style magician and con man). In any case, Mike goes to the bathroom, the guy twists his ring, and when he comes back, the shrink tells Mike about it. Sure that the other guy is bluffing, the psychiatrist agrees to back Mike's bet when he's raised over what cash he has at the table—but Mike loses. The other guy pulls a gun, and the psychiatrist starts to write a check . . . when the gun starts leaking water on the table. It turns out the whole thing was a con from the beginning, and everyone is in on it but the psychiatrist; just the first twist in a multileveled con game of a great movie (plus Mamet's dialogue always rocks!).

Steve Badger (professional poker player). *Kaleidoscope* (1966) is an obscure, pre–*Bonnie and Clyde* Warren Beatty film. Beatty breaks into a factory and doctors the plates that print the cards used by the major casinos of the world. He marks the cards in a way only he can see. Naturally, after these cards go into circulation, Beatty goes on the rush to end all rushes playing blackjack and poker. Unfortunately for him, when forced into a head-up no-limit game, they switch cards to ones he can't read. Now forced to play using only his wits, he traps his opponent into an enormous pot—only to be faced with the best poker decision I've seen in a movie. Check it out. *[Editor's note: also check out Steve's article on poker movies at www.playwinning poker.com.]*

Kelly Kuvo (performance artist). In *Westworld* (1973), the poker game is the "ain't we a couple of stinkers with shit-eating grins?"–turning point when the two human characters realize that they have paid for and can now legally live out their sick fantasy that all men are just groovy evil testosterone-pumped sex machines. They therefore play cards in a Wild West saloon with a bunch of robot cowboys, cheat at the game, start a drunken brawl, shoot to kill, and then go upstairs and bone a couple of robot whores. It's incredible, it's nasty, and it's lame . . . I love it!

Jon Tamblin (special-effects technician). *Futureworld* (1976) is a sort-of sequel to the amazing *Westworld*, but in spirit this is much closer to the low-budget evil-robot movies *KISS Meets the Phantom of the Park* and *Halloween III*. The best moment of the film is where lovable robot technician Harry (Stuart Margolin, who played Angel in *The Rockford Files*) relaxes by playing poker with a faceless robot. Talk about a poker face!

Rob Coffy (Web master, CombustibleCelluloid.com). It's kind of a guilty pleasure, but I really get a bang out of the big climactic scene in *Rounders* (1998), in which Matt Damon plays John Malkovich for everything he has. The way Malkovich snarls that line "Lays down a monster" really gets me.

John Morgan (communications director). *Butch Cassidy and the Sundance Kid* (1969)—opening sequence. Gambler accuses Sundance of cheating. Butch asks Gambler to apologize. Gambler refuses. Butch says, "Well, I can't help ya, Sundance." Gambler says, "I didn't know you were the Sundance Kid when I accused you of cheating." Butch says, "Well, it'd be like suicide drawing on Sundance," so he should apologize and ask them to stay. Gambler apologizes, Sundance takes the pot, and as he's walking away, the Gambler says—"Hey, how fast are you?" Butch dodges the table and Sundance opens fire. It was a touching moment.

Meg Rabinowitz (teacher). There is something awesome about the way the men talk to one another in the poker scenes in *In the Bedroom* (2001). The way they gently chide each other along is very appealing, and it establishes relationships and characters quickly. I love the guy who sings or recites poetry as a delay tactic. And then, when the emotional ante is raised in the film and a critical character is lost, the conversation between the men is incredibly healing and transformative for the male lead in the film, played by Tom Wilkinson. I am also a fan of the *Ocean's Eleven* remake (2001) and the poker scene where Brad Pitt is tutoring young celebrities who want to learn to play the game. This is a hilarious scene that demonstrates who is schooling whom when George Clooney shows up and takes a turn with Pitt's students.

Eric Nix (blacksmith). *Shanghai Noon* (2000) is a terrible movie, but there is a memorable poker scene, mainly because it culminates in a Jackie Chan action sequence (though not a very good Jackie Chan action sequence). Chan plays Chon, who finds himself in the Old West trying to save a Chinese princess. He soon exposes his soon-to-be-buddy Roy (Owen Wilson) as a crooked cardplayer when he notices him cheating at poker by using a retracting card feeder hidden in his sleeve. The ensuing action sequence is disappointing, because Chan misses an opportunity to use cards and chips and a retracting card feeder as weapons in the brawl.

Dan Sutherland (independent filmmaker). I worked on this movie that had a poker scene in it. It is called *Under the Influence*. Shot in L.A. in 1997 for $150,000, it's finally out of hock and near a distribution deal. The poker scene is stock: main characters, the foils, and some day players are up all night drinking booze and playing poker. The actors are all women. The scene is intense because it is at an assistant district attorney's house, and the protagonist—a woman involved in murder and insurance fraud—has insinuated herself into the table. The dialogue is fairly banal; it's an introduction scene to the D.A. and her pals. The technical things that make a poker scene at a round table work are all here: 1. The eyeline. Where are the actors looking? Their cards, each other—where is their focus and how does a director "cover" this to make it work? 2. The art direction. This is the ephemera and minutiae you are not supposed to notice. Why? Because it distracts you from the drama. This could be—for the poker game—the cards, the cigarette(s) (how long is the burn, what kind, the ashtray's contents), the drinks—all of these little details have to be watched over intently, because what might play for ninety seconds on screen takes two nights to shoot. 3. Energy. Most of these scenes are shot out-of-sequence and then assembled in postproduction. So, you would have an actor who does all of her dialogue in close-ups, and the intensity has to match the script. She might be curious in one shot and then focused in the next, and bluffing in the third. This is even harder in poker scenes because you have people playing characters who are bluffing. A poker scene is a real test of a director's skill and an actor's ability.

Barbara Holt (screenwriter). It's 1965, the big talent show is in full swing, and the doo-wop group next up on stage is missing its two lead singers, Bobby and Eddie. Cut to a back-alley poker game, and there these guys are, trying to steal a pot from two old Turks. Caught in the act, they are forced to crash out of a window and run desperately for their lives. Bobby is disabled by their pursuers, but Eddie makes it to the theater just in time to slide dramatically on stage and grab the mic. Oh, the hand Eddie held that gave them away? Eddie was holding two aces of hearts. Maybe that extra card is why the group, and the film about them, were called *The Five Heartbeats* (1991).

Natasha Morgan (film buff). I think my favorite poker scene is the Girl Scouts playing poker in *Airplane!* (1980), and the fight that ensues (and ensues and ensues) . . . .

Sergio Mims (film critic). In *Beverly Hills Cop III* (1994), Eddie Murphy walks into a back room at an amusement park and a bunch of mascots in oversized animal costumes are playing cards. It's like a life-size recreation of one of those "dogs playing poker" paintings. It's the only funny shot in the whole movie.

Waymon Timbsdayle (music critic). *The Odd Couple* (1968) features the absolute best neighborhood poker scene ever in a movie. The guys gather at the spacious apartment of slovenly sportswriter Oscar Madison (brilliantly grimaced by Walter Matthau), only to have the game unintentionally sabotaged by Oscar's new roommate, the Martha Stewart-esque Felix Unger. Felix (Jack Lemmon) is a compulsive cleaner, who can't help but turn every action by the players into a juggling act of coasters, dust rags, and disinfectant. He also insists on coordinating the snacks, and soon the dynamic of the poker table separates the men from the not-so-men. One of the manly players ultimately quits because, due to Felix's fastidiousness, "in the last three hours we've played four minutes of poker." However, the two more emasculated players eventually are won over by Felix's exquisite finger sandwiches, delighted that he cuts off the crusts. The game ends when the surviving macho man (who has been vehemently arguing that a sterile environment is anti-poker) smells some antiseptic and realizes that Felix has *washed the cards*. Though they don't really get to play, this scene says loads about the dynamic of guys interacting at the poker table (and having to deal with that one annoying guy).

Bohus Blahut (filmmaker). Weird Al Yankovic's film *UHF* (1989) has a considerable cult following today given its limited theatrical run (though I saw it in the theater six times). Weird Al has made his mark with his clever parodies of top-charting pop tunes, so it's logical that his film outing would spoof countless TV and film genres. It is this that makes me think of what elements make up the typical gangster-movie poker scene. The setting is a round table, scattered with pretzels and playing cards, in a moody warehouse. Smoke is vaguely in the air, though no one is smoking, and there are a few shafts of dramatic light. The tough guys don't actually play as much as rearrange the cards in their hands and talk about what they're going to do next. There's also something about a warehouse full of tall piles of clean cardboard boxes that tells you that stuntmen will be whipping around soon. The Weird Al touches include one of the baddies preferring to play jacks, and the lead goon being deathly afraid of bugs. While not exactly a pivotal scene in the movie, it does let you see how few visual elements it takes to make the viewer think "seedy card game."

Art Fein (cable-access producer). I have a most-hated poker scene in a movie, and that is in the Disney remake of *The Parent Trap* (1998). It infuriated me on two different levels. A guy says that one of the girls is "the hot poker player at camp." Well, these are all nine-year-old girls—this is ridiculous to begin with. They might play cards, but *poker* doesn't exist unless you have money. But I tried to suspend my disbelief. Then at some point, the twins face each other at poker, they're still not friends, and one says, "I got four of a kind" and the other says "I have a royal flush." Somebody writing this movie thinks you can play well by getting a hand. That's ridiculous. Playing is a continuous thing, not, "look, I can walk in and get four of a kind, watch." And the other part of my objection is that the twins hold the cards up to the camera. You've got kids in the audience under ten watching this, they don't know what the hell's going on. No eight-year-old is going to know what a royal flush is. Ridiculous hubris on the part of the writers.

everything I ever needed to know about poker I learned from Honeymoon in Vegas

by Pete Fornatale

W ITH ALL DUE RESPECT to many of the fine writers who've written indispensable instructional poker books over the years, from Mike Caro to David Sklansky to John Scarne, I want to offer up another fine source of poker knowledge: *Honeymoon in Vegas*.

The film was directed by Andrew Bergman, who wrote *The In-Laws* (1979) and also directed *The Freshman*, which launched the comedy dream team of Matthew Broderick, Marlon Brando, and a Komodo Dragon. But to me, Bergman's finest work came in 1992 with a combination paean to Elvis and unintentional poker primer.

Honeymoon in Vegas is an underrated movie with something for everyone, from the now-famous Flying Elvises to a brilliant comedic performance by James Caan to Bruce Springsteen singing "Viva Las Vegas." But none of that really matters to the poker player. What matters is the film's best scene, the poker sequence that sets up the film's plot. Here's the deal: Tommy Korman (the aforementioned Caan) sees Jack and Betsy (Nicolas Cage and Sarah Jessica Parker) on the casino floor and falls hard for Betsy, who is a dead ringer for his late wife. Knowing he needs to get Jack out of the picture, he arranges to invite him to a private game. What I love about this scene is all the gambling truths one can learn from watching it.

1. Don't play out of your league.

Jack's big mistake was getting into that game in the first place. To gamble well, you need to be in a mental comfort zone. You need an environment that's going to promote a winning attitude. If you're used to playing nickel, dime, quarter, even just the raise in stakes to quarter, fifty, dollar can throw you off your game. If you're used to playing with publishing types on a makeshift card table where it's tough to lose $50 in a night, and then you end up around a felt-covered poker table with clay chips, playing with mortgage traders who think nothing of losing that much in a hand, look out, play tight, and go home early.

Even if you're a better-than-average home game player, if you get in a private game where you're suddenly in too deep, or if you decide to try your luck in the casino, odds are that your decision-making skills are going to suffer.

2. The best games involve a cast of diverse characters.

Set aside for a moment Tommy Korman's motives for luring Jack into his private game and his secret desire to go Sonny Corleone on his ass. The man knows how to put a game together. He's got a guy named Tony Cataracts in there, played by Seymour Cassel (known to many as Max's father in *Rushmore*, he's the type of working actor about whom you'll definitely say "I know that guy!" even if you don't know where from). There's the brilliant cameo of Jerry Tarkanian as Sid Feder (Tark the Shark, of course, coached the infamous UNLV Running Rebels, and seemed a natural as a degenerate cardplayer).

My personal favorite is the Asian Elvis impersonator who sits in on the game—in character.

One key to putting together a good game is trying to find people from different walks of life, with different backgrounds, who like to play different games. It's more interesting and creates a better dynamic. The best game I ever played in was with one friend from work who was new to the game, one degenerate gambler from back home, my fastidious roommate, the neighborhood cop—wait, that wasn't me, that was Oscar Madison in *The Odd Couple*. Seriously, though, if you get a group of guys from the same industry, there's too much of a tendency for mah jongg–esque shop talk that would be better around a water cooler than a poker table.

3. There's no such thing as "unbeatable."

Jack ends up betting out on a straight flush to the jack, only to be beat by Tommy's straight flush to the queen. He loses $65,000. Of course, Tommy conveniently has a better solution. If Jack lets him spend a weekend with Betsy in Kauai, the debt will be forgiven. She is forced to acquiesce as Jack asks her, "Do you know what a straight flush is? It's like . . . unbeatable." She counters, "'Like unbeatable' is not unbeatable."

And therein lies one of the great poker truisms. You can never bet what you can not afford to lose, even if the odds say you should normally take the chance. Even if you're pretty sure you've got your opponent beat, if you've made the mistake of betting more than you have, you're going to come out a loser sometime—probably sooner rather than later.

And sometimes it's not a question of *literally* betting what you don't have, just more of a psychological threshold you don't want to cross. If you're mentally prepared to lose $100 and you lose twice that, it's going to sour you a bit and affect your all-important winning mind-set. Once that's lost, forget the $200—you could be in a lot more trouble than that.

4. If it looks like a setup, it probably is.

Naturally, Tommy's little game wasn't exactly on the up-and-up. And there were some clues Jack should have picked up on. The odds against getting a straight flush are 72,193 to 1. To be invited into a private game by a professional gambler and suddenly have this miracle hand dealt your way. . . . Suffice to say he should have smelled a rat. And while I have never been cold-decked personally, I've heard a lot of stories about suspicious deals, phony rules, and out-and-out larceny. Stay in tune with your surroundings. A friend of mine once had two of his regulars cancel at the last minute. So to make seven, he wound up inviting some friend of a friend and *his* fat buddy with bad facial hair. During the game, he noticed the two new guys tapping the table and touching their faces and otherwise signaling to each other. . . . Let's just say they weren't invited back.

If you're ever in a situation where you sense things don't look copacetic, get out fast. Sure, you might not wind up losing your fiancée, chasing her to Hawaii, getting scammed by Arnold from *Happy Days*, and skydiving in an Elvis-style American Eagle jumpsuit to win her back, like Jack Singer did. But you're pretty damn sure to lose your shirt. And a good poker shirt is hard to find.

KNOW WHEN TO FOLD 'EM

POKER AS A COUNTRY-MUSIC METAPHOR.

by Ken Burke

ALTHOUGH it definitely takes a backseat to drinking, divorce, truck driving, and jingoistic rebellion, gambling—particularly poker—has been a reliable staple of country music. From Tex Williams's "Downtown Poker Club" and Tex Ritter's "Jack o' Diamonds" to Jerry Reed's "Uptown Poker Club" and Juice Newton's "Queen of Hearts," there have been dozens of Southern-fried card-oriented songs that have served as catalysts for low comedy, sentimentality, wisdom, and, especially, romance. Below, in no particular order, are dissections of a few of them.

The Gambler

Perhaps the most famous poker song of all time, the 1978 hit (#1 C&W, #16 Pop) made Kenny Rogers a country crossover superstar, leading to a series of woodenly acted made-for-TV movies and a pretty decent chicken franchise. The ditty, in which a gambler offers to exchange advice for a last swallow of whiskey (always a fair trade), was initially recorded by its author, Don Schlitz, who also cowrote such mammoth country hits as "On the Other Hand," "Forever and

Ever, Amen," and "He Thinks He'll Keep Her." Schlitz's version exhibited none of Larry Butler's deft production skills or Rogers's world-weary vocal charm, but it provided a helluva blueprint.

Indeed, legendary Nashville producer Billy Sherrill, who engineered Rogers's version of "The Gambler," told Dan Daley of *Mix Online*, "It was one of those songs everyone just knew was going to be a hit. Fortunately it had 'Kenny Rogers' written all over it." Butler accented the acoustic guitar rhythm, cut the track live in a small one-room studio, later redubbing Rogers's craggy vocal, and crafted a hit around a hook line that still resonates today ("You got to know when to hold 'em, know when to fold 'em," etc.).

You'll notice that the song offers no specifics on *how* you'll know when to hold 'em or fold 'em. That's because that type of wisdom is revealed to different card players, in a variety of ways, at different points in their card-playing lives. However, the metaphoric advice is clear. In order to be a success in life, you should learn to trust yourself, react intuitively, and have the good sense to haul ass to save ass. And for crying out loud, don't engage in unseemly gloating; it gives your enemies a good reason to bust your chops. Sound advice, well worth taking.

That said, a late 2002 report claimed that Rogers plans to star in even more "Gambler" TV films, proving conclusively that, while the song's greatest interpreter may know how to hold 'em, he sure doesn't know when to fold 'em.

Deal

Tom T. Hall, country's best singer-songwriter of the 1970s, eschewed his usual drawn-from-true-life storytelling technique in favor of some uplifting pasteboard-related philosophy for this 1975 #8 hit. When life gets too tough, the Kentucky-born hitmaker recommends the following: "*Deal!* Maybe the next card's an ace!" It is not only a credo that keeps card players at the table, but an encapsulation of the tacit foolish hopes all humans must keep alive in order to get out of bed in the morning. What other choice do we have but to keep trying and hope for the best?

Hall warns, however, that how you play the game is important too, as there may be ramifications to violating a card player's ethical code: "It won't do to cheat, because you have to cash in when you die."

So, you haven't won the love of your life? You fail at every ambitious undertaking? You're regretting a missed opportunity? Hall tries to comfort us with a reminder of the cyclical nature of both poker and life: "The good thing about life is they shuffle and they deal life again." Whether he is talking about reincarnation or proffering the paranoid notion that our destinies are being controlled by not one, but many unseen forces is not clear. But his lyrical mastery of life's wisdom as it relates to card play is simple, direct, and amusing.

A perky harmonica-laden novelty, "Deal" is a relatively minor song in Hall's canon, one of his forty-one Top-40 country hits between 1967 and 1984. However, it smartly bookends the more bitter pontifications of his other hit gambling allusion, "Faster Horses" (#1, 1976), wherein a cynical cowboy admonishes an idealistic poet that life is all about "faster horses, younger women, older whiskey, more *money*!"

Hall, who fashioned all his best work for producer Jerry Kennedy at Mercury Records, opted for "more money" when he made the switch to RCA in 1977. It was a card he should have never played. Although he was blessed with a few more hits, the truthful feel of his songs was compromised by slicker production values. As a result, his chart momentum slowed noticeably. A belated return to Mercury in 1984 sparked one last gasp of popularity before Hall reshuffled his priorities and went into semiretirement.

Five-Card Stud

During the 1960s, producer Jimmy Bowen helped transform Italian pop crooner Dean Martin into the King of Ersatz Country. Although

Martin didn't officially release a country album until 1983, he and
Bowen filled their Reprise LPs with dozens of country standards
such as Eddy Arnold's "Welcome to My World" and Merle Haggard's
"I Take a Lot of Pride in Who I Am." Intended for adult contemporary playlists, these smooth, heartfelt recordings would probably be
deemed "too country" by modern country-music programmers.

Recorded for the soundtrack of the 1968 movie of the same
name, "Five Card Stud" is notable for two reasons: 1. Without the
burden of Bowen's usual corny arrangement sense, Martin proved
to be as authentic-sounding a western balladeer as Frankie Laine or
Marty Robbins. 2. Martin clearly reveled in singing a song whose
character was suspiciously close to his own: "Liked his gals and fun,
anted up and run—run right back to five-card stud."

The movie itself was a thin western/mystery, with Robert
Mitchum playing a groggy version of his *Night of the Hunter*
preacher, a miscast Roddy McDowall wildly overacting, and Martin
apparently reading his lines off cue cards. Worst of all? There just
weren't enough scenes with the singer manipulating cards and tossing chips. When you consider that Dino had once been a professional
dealer, and that he often dealt blackjack between sets of his shows
in Vegas, the missed chance to watch him make good on the following boast seems unforgivable: "When he played, he played for
blood—he was king at five-card stud."

Deck of Cards

The story of a soldier brought up on charges of using a deck of cards
during church services was the most famous recitation record of the
post–World War II era. Indeed, hit versions of "Deck of Cards" have
been released by T. Texas Tyler (#2 C&W, 1948), Tex Ritter (#10
C&W, 1948), and Wink Martindale (#7 pop, #11 C&W, 1959), and
the text has been included in countless inspirational collections.

It's important to note that card and dice cheats in the armed
forces were a serious wartime problem, and a difficult one to combat.

Frontline soldiers needed something to quell the tumultuous mix of fear, fatigue, and boredom they experienced between battles. In most cases, officers and noncoms just looked the other way as long as the card play wasn't too obvious. In that light, spreading out a deck of cards wasn't just a blatant affront to church-service decorum, it was a knee-jerk act of rebellion and military disrespect.

It has long been assumed that this story of a young soldier's defense of his deck of cards was religious testimony. Read in cold print, with a healthy dose of modern day cynicism, however, the soldier's rationale plays out like the practiced con of an experienced card shark.

Each card contains an appropriate religious reference, explains the soldier. The ace reminds him "that there is but one God." The three represents "the Father, the Son, and the Holy Spirit." The four is "Matthew, Mark, Luke, and John." Moving from card to card, the soldier increasingly imbues his defense with the irreproachable piety of a backwoods bible-school teacher. Finally, lest his interrogator think him an unmanageable zealot, he likens the numerical properties of his cards to an almanac, proving both the versatility of his controversial possession and the powers of his faith.

Today we'd suspect that the soldier in question is clearly a poker player out-bluffing the provost marshal with a lot of smooth talk. After all, who is more facile with scripture-based analogies than a con man? In fact, it wouldn't be hard for a modern audience to mentally fast-forward the soldier's life to a time when he might be dealing three-card monte with a religious twist. "OK! OK! OK! We got three cards here—the Son of God, the Virgin Mary, and the King of Kings. Take a good look at the King of Kings! Lay the cards face down! I switch 'em this way; I switch 'em that way! Now you, sir, find the King of Kings! Ten'll get you twenty if you can find the King of Kings!"

Yet the era when "Deck of Cards" was originally released was populated by less suspicious people and less ironic artists, generally speaking. The recitation was intended to foster the notion that spirituality can be found anywhere, and that's how it was taken.

During the dramatic payoff for the soldier's successful defense, the narrator assures us his intentions were pure, adding, " . . . friends, this story is true. I know . . . I was that soldier."

Or was he?

Tillman Franks of the Louisiana Hayride knew and liked Tyler, the listed author of "Deck of Cards." "He had a lot of charisma," Franks explained. When asked if Tyler's story was indeed based on true experiences, Franks answered, "No, I don't think it was true, though he used that line his entire life."

But was it his line to use?

Northwest rockabilly pioneer Bobby Wayne heard a different story about the song's origins from a member of Tyler's band in 1954. "Lloyd 'Dug' Dugger was a bass player for T. Texas Tyler," recalled Wayne, "and he told me they found that song, a poem really, in somebody's attic. As I understood it, it was actually a letter written to one of Tyler's relatives somewhere back east from a guy in the military." Wayne's childhood friend, the late Gary Bryant, toured with his hero Tyler in 1953, and had heard the same story.

Regardless of authorship or poetic license, Tyler was a World War II veteran whose personable approach made his testimony seem authentic, and "Deck of Cards" made him a star. Dubbed "The Man with a Million Friends," the former David Luke Myrick parlayed his newfound notoriety into a brief career in western movies, a regular Los Angeles TV series, and a small string of hit records. "Out west, he was way more popular than Hank Williams," remembers Wayne, who saw him perform several times. "He could start talking to someone at the side of the stage, and people would crowd around to listen to him, and you could hear a pin drop. People just loved him."

Warmly acted, Ritter's rendition of "Deck of Cards" was just one of many major hits he enjoyed during his lifetime. Martindale's comparatively bland retelling (a major seller with '50s teens and their parents) was his only smash. Both performers enjoyed continued success into the autumn of their lives (Ritter in music, Martindale as a perennial TV game-show host).

By contrast, Tyler was in dire financial straits and sodden with drink during his later years. Franks recalled that 4 Star label honcho Bill McCall exacerbated a lot of Tyler's problems by not paying him for his hits. "Bill McCall never paid nobody. He was about as bad as they come that way."

Tyler's state of affairs got so bad that Franks once had to borrow fifty dollars from a loan company so the singer could leave town. Fortunately, it didn't end that way. The last time Franks saw him, Tyler (perhaps taking a cue from "Deck of Cards") had sobered up, become a preacher, and retrofitted some of his songs to accommodate gospel lyrics. He recorded forty of them, just vocal and guitar, on an LP that he gave in exchange for offerings at revivals. One of those albums was the only repayment Franks ever got for his fifty bucks.

Although he could ill afford the debt at the time, the thought of which still irritates his long-suffering wife, Franks never regretted making the loan. "Sometimes you have to take a chance on a friend."

Tyler died in 1972.

Mother, the Queen of My Heart

Jerry Lee Lewis recorded two versions of this sentimental Jimmie Rodgers song about a loving son who forsakes his sainted mother's dying wish and indulges in the twin vices of drinking and gambling.

The first rendition appeared during Lewis's country comeback peak on his 1971 Mercury LP *Touching Home*. Despite superb vocalizing, Lewis's performance seemed little more than anachronistic album filler. It was at a 1987 session, in songwriter Hank Cochran's basement studio, that the Killer fully mined the shame of his primal oedipal conflict.

At the behest of his friend, "Meat Man"–songwriter Mack Vickery, Lewis showed up at Cochran's home studio, ostensibly to cut a gospel album. The results were eventually released on the European import *At Hank Cochran's* (Trend, 1995). Playing on a rickety synthesizer, the Ferriday Fireball plumbed his memory for such chestnuts as "Won't You Ride in My Little Red Wagon," "Mammy," "Melancholy Baby," "Mexicali Rose," and "Beautiful Dreamer." With the synthesizer adding cartoonish Caribbean rhythms, metronome-type percussion, and woodwind keyboard effects, this experimental curiosity could've easily been titled *The Killer Sings Karaoke*.

Lewis ditched the intrusive F/X, however, for a nakedly expressive turn at "Mother, the Queen of My Heart." Changing tempos nearly every verse, imbuing his vocals with whiskey-gargling half-yodels and spoken asides, the fallen superstar employed Rodgers's song as a 3-minute, 23-second metaphor for his lifetime of reckless drinking and suicidal career missteps: "Jerry Lee would bet his clothes and his money, never dreaming that I'd ever fall."

Singing with the hunger of a poker veteran whose eyes are on an especially large pot, Lewis poignantly testifies, "All I needed to break 'em was one card, and that was a queen." The luck of the draw seemingly provides the ultimate triumph. In the pasteboard queen's visage, however, the compulsive gambler detects the disappointed face of his darling mother, and the image has a sobering impact.

Like his friend and rival Elvis Presley, Lewis held his mother in high regard, and her admonitions were the only ones the famed piano pumper ever seriously heeded. So, as he sings, "I saw my mama's picture. Somehow it seemed to say, 'Son, you have broken your promise,'" is it any wonder we hear rock 'n' roll's original bad boy wince with guilt?

At song's end, the reformed gambler and recalcitrant rocker are one, as the weepy declaration is made: "I'll never forget that promise to my mother; she was the queen of my old heart."

"Now *that's* great," exclaimed the engineer. Having survived a confrontation with his true essence, a relieved and penitent Lewis agrees.

From a Jack to a King

Ned Miller is something of a mystery man. His 1963 smash (#6 Pop, #2 country, #2 U.K.) was the ultimate poker-as-romance metaphor. A talented songwriter, Miller penned "Dark Moon" for Bonnie Guitar (#14 C&W, #6 Pop, 1957) and Gale Storm (#4 Pop, 1957), and "A Fallen Star" for Jimmy C. Newman (#2 C&W, 1957). The Utah-born singer-songwriter had a small string of country Top-40 hits including "Invisible Tears" (#13 C&W, 1964) and "Do What You Do Do Well" (#7 C&W, #52 Pop, 1964). Yet little is known or divulged about his whereabouts today. All we have is the music, and maybe that's how it should be.

Fabor Robinson initially leased Miller's recording of his composition "From a Jack to a King" to Dot Records in 1957, where it failed miserably. Smoother versions by Jim Reeves and Jim Lowe of "Green Door" fame didn't fare any better. Five years later, for reasons still unknown, Robinson reissued Miller's recording on his own Fabor label.

Sung with a needy hillbilly vibrato that nearly skitters off pitch, Miller's bouncy shuffle championed the use of backroom poker connivance as a romantic strategy: "With no regrets I stacked the cards last night, and lady luck played her hand just right."

Apparently the lady in question was a pretty fair bluffer, although the singer's poker acumen eventually allows him to spot the ultimate "tell": "For just a little while I thought that I might lose the game; then just in time I saw the twinkle in your eye."

A mammoth hit upon rerelease, "From a Jack to a King" has been a staple of TV-advertised country compilations ever since. Moreover, throughout the years the song has been covered by dozens of artists—Elvis Presley got off a particularly bluesy version, and it was successfully revived by Ricky Van Shelton (#1 C&W, 1989).

This writer wanted to speak to Miller about how poker impacted the creation of his song, but the former pipe fitter and taxicab driver was nowhere to be found. Countless inquiries proved futile. Finally, Richard Davis, personal manager to Little Jimmy Dickens and Ferlin Husky, made a call on my behalf to Frances Preston, president of BMI in New York.

Preston called Jamie Music in Philadelphia and discovered that a "flag" existed on Miller's account. It seems no one is allowed to get directly in touch with Ned Miller. Those making inquiries are instructed to send a letter in care of the publishing house, and Miller may or may not get in touch.

In this case, he did not.

One of the last performers to remember seeing Miller was country superstar Bobby Bare; they were both at Central Songs from 1961 through 1964. Miller came to one of Bare's shows during the 1980s in "Montana or Wyoming or something—Utah, or wherever." The onetime friends exchanged greetings; that's all Bare can remember. It was a long time ago.

However, Bare did shed some light on why Miller, in his mid-seventies as of this writing, chooses to be inaccessible. "He didn't consider himself an entertainer. He never thought of himself as a singer—he just wasn't cut out for show business. He didn't like any part of it. He was just a songwriter and that's all he wanted to be."

Richard Davis validated Bare's recollection. "I had a few minor business dealings with Ned and he was very difficult to deal with. Everything about the business irritated him. He'd say, 'Why do I have to do this? I'm a *songwriter*.'"

Miller also complained to Davis that Fabor Robinson severely shortchanged him on "From a Jack to a King," paying him between $50 and $250 for that monster international hit record. According to Bare, those types of complaints about Robinson are nothing new.

Many believe Miller damaged his own career by refusing to do promotional tours—it seems he was afflicted with severe attacks of stage fright.

One published report claimed that Ned Miller had retired to Las Vegas. The folks at Jamie Music say that isn't so; this writer believes them. After all, Vegas would've been too ironic a resting place for a man who apparently couldn't recognize a winning hand when it was dealt to him.

rock 'n' roll poker poems

by Waymon Timbsdayle

Illustration by Jerome Gaynor

Rock 'n' Roll Busted Flush

Motörhead—"Ace of Spades"
Peetie Wheatstraw—"King of Spades"
Styx—"Queen of Spades"
Boogie Down Productions—"Jack of Spades"

Stacy Q—"Two of Hearts"

Rock 'n' Roll Misdeal

Angelic Upstarts—"Ace of Hearts"
KISS—"King of Hearts"
Bob Dylan—"Rosemary and the Jack of Hearts"
Whitesnake—"Queen of Hearts"

Juice Newton—"Queen of Hearts"

The Rock 'n' Roll Nuts

Awkward Star—"10 of Diamonds"
The Byrds—"Jack of Diamonds"
Roy Brown—"The Queen of Diamonds"
Spirit Gum—"Ace of Diamonds"

KING DIAMOND!

◆ *King Diamond* ◆

Poker in Literature

by Jake Austen

PART OF POKER'S APPEAL is based on its rough-and-tumble associations with illiterate cowboy and mobster lowlifes. Despite this, players covet poker books. Rule books and instructional manuals have been around almost as long as the game, and many players value them like a stack of blue chips. Poker players are a remarkably studious lot, willing to cram like a college student, and excited to read their favorite authors. Despite being a motivated readership, players put little importance on the literary value of the books in their poker libraries. Fiction writers have responded to this indifference by visiting card themes less often than one would expect. But when poker and literature do intersect, it is interesting to see what writers do with a game so steeped in drama, fantasy, and surprise endings. As the history of poker books plays itself out, perhaps the best table to be sitting at is the one where the pragmatic aspects of poker writing square off against the game's own literary possibilities.

The history of poker books is somewhat muddled from its start, since the most famous and oft-quoted poker writer actually died before poker was invented. London's Edmund Hoyle (1672–1769) gained fame for his pamphlets that gave systematic instructions for whist and other games. His reputation outlived him, and the world's

most popular series of rule books are still published under the
"Hoyle" name. But even his posthumous authority on poker is ques-
tionable. Poker seems to have come into existence in the early 1830s,
but *Hoyle's* doesn't mention the game until its 1850 and 1857 editions, both of which describe it briefly and inaccurately. Poker is not
properly featured until the 1867 edition, decades after Jonathan H.
Green described poker in print in *An Exposure of the Arts and Mis-
eries of Gambling* (1843). To this day various editions of *Hoyle's* are
cited as definitive poker reference books, but their supremacy has
been challenged in the pages of John Scarne's poker guides. Cardsharp Scarne was offended at the authority bestowed upon a man
dead seventy years before poker's birth. In *Scarne's Guide to Modern Poker* (1979), he indulges his fantasies of grandeur by stating that
the phrase "according to Hoyle" has been replaced by "according to
Scarne."

Perhaps the most literate titles in the poker bookworm's collection are dramatic memoirs, biographies, and journalistic accounts of
famed gamblers and legendary games. The classic *The Education of
a Poker Player* by Herbert O. Yardley (1957), the masterful *The
Biggest Game* in Town by A. Alvarez (1983), the amusing *Big Deal* by
Anthony Holden (1990), and the witty *Poker Nation* by Andy Bellin
(2002) are as fun to read as any novel. But as readable as they are,
these firsthand accounts differ from standard plot-oriented narratives. Poker readers demand instruction and guides to improvement
from their literature, so these books often depart into formulas,
charts, and methodical descriptions of card play in ways totally anti-
thetical to the writerly voice the authors employ in the rest of the text.

Those formulas and charts make up the bulk of the most popular poker books, the instructional manuals that put literary aspira-
tions aside and get down to the business of teaching readers how to
win. These books range in quality and tone, from rudimentary and
practical to bold and colorful to downright evil (see "Poker For Bas-

tards," Dan Kelly's essay herein on Frank R. Wallace's *Poker: A Guaranteed Income for Life by Using the Advanced Concepts of Poker*). Seminal titles in this genre include *Super/System (a Course in Power Poker)* by Doyle Brunson (1978), *Caro's Book of Tells: The Body Language of Poker* by the "Mad Genius of Poker," Mike Caro (1984), *The Theory of Poker* by David Sklansky (1987), and *Poker: A Winner's Guide* by Andy Nelson (1996). Fascinatingly, the writers of these tomes, unlike an auto manual's author, are expected to prove their mettle. When James McManus made it to the finals of the World Series of Poker in 2000, as chronicled in his compelling memoir *Positively Fifth Street* (2003), he found himself seated next to T. J. Cloutier, who just happened to write *Championship No-Limit & Pot-Limit Hold 'Em* (1997), the "bible" McManus studied daily to prepare himself for the tournament. (It is notable that "bible" author Cloutier eventually lost the tournament to a player named Jesus.)

Though the previously mentioned guides make the poker section at Borders bulge, poker themes are rarer in fiction. Many dramatic poker sequences occur in "low" popular literature, their titles often better known for their film adaptations. For example, there's an excellent poker sequence in James Jones's *From Here to Eternity* (1951). *The Cincinnati Kid*, by Richard Jessup (1963), is as compelling a tale of a poker hustler as its cinematic spawn. And the card games James Bond plays (though they're more often bridge or baccarat than poker) are more prominent in print than on the silver screen (most notably with his victory over evil industrialist Hugo Drax in Ian Fleming's *Moonraker*, 1955). Poker also was as prominent in western pulp fiction as it was in western B-movies. From penny dreadfuls to dime novels, thousands of poker scenes appeared in countless titles, including *Deadwood Dick's Doom* by Edward L. Wheeler (1899) and Max Brand's *Destry Rides Again* (1930).

Poker scenes are less common in more "serious" fiction. An exception is a brief, lyrical hand of poker played to decide the ownership of

a slave in William Faulkner's *Go Down Moses* (1942). In that
sequence, in which poker play is portrayed as a dire, ritualistic activity, Faulkner has a character refer to the game as "the most serious
foolishness you ever took part in in your life." There may be more
classic poker scenes in the future, as a new breed of poker novels (by
men *and* women) has recently emerged. These page-turners include
King of the Small World by Rick Bennett (1995), *Stone Cold* (1999)
by Pete Hautman, and *Girls' Poker Night: A Novel* by Jill A. Davis
(2002).

Perhaps the best moments of poker in literature do not rely on
the high drama of a poker showdown. Rather, poker culture is often
mined for its characters, its mood, and even its equipment. Mark
Twain and Bret Harte romanticized the gamblers of poker's most
storied era without getting into the game play. The cardsharp
Oakhurst and the rest of Harte's "Outcasts of Poker Flat" (1869)
have lives determined by their poker pasts and their gambler's luck,
but the only time cards appear in the story is when Oakhurst writes
his suicide note on the deuce of clubs. In a biting social satire, Ray
Bradbury wrote not about a poker game, but about a poker chip: in
"The Watchful Poker Eye of H. Matisse" (1954), an attention seeker
has Henri Matisse paint a blue eye on a poker chip, and wears it in
lieu of a glass eye or eyepatch. Eventually sheeplike in-crowds around
the world use reproductions of his "eye" in home poker games.

My favorite poker passage isn't about the game at all, but about
the powers and mystique of an X-rated deck of playing cards. In
Jonathan Safran Foer's *Everything Is Illuminated* (2002), a Jewish
American writer searches the Ukraine for a woman who may have
saved his grandfather from the Nazis. He invents a folkloric history
of his grandfather's shtetl, from its naming in 1791 to its inescapable
extermination in 1942. In the following passage, he imagines his
grandfather as a boy, a prolific lothario whose crippled arm possesses
the power to make women of all ages fall in love with him.

But before the portrait is painted too flatteringly, it should be mentioned that widows comprised only half of my young grandfather's
lovers. He lived a double life: lover of not only grievers, but women
untouched by grief's damp hand, those closer to their first death than
their second. There were some fifty-two virgins, to whom he made
love in each of the positions that he had studied from a deck of dirty
cards, loaned to him by a friend whom he kept leaving at the theater:
sixty-nining the one-eyed jack Tali M, with tight pigtails and folded-
yarmulke eye patch; taking from behind the two of hearts Brandil W,
who had only one very weak heart, which made her hobble and wear
thick spectacles, and who died before the war—too early, and just
early enough; spoons with queen of diamonds Mella S, all breasts and
no backside, the only daughter of the wealthiest family in Kolki (who,
they say, would never use silverware more than once); mounted by the
ace of spades Trema O, most diligent in the fields, whose shrieks, he
was sure, would give them away. They loved him and he fucked
them—ten, jack, queen, king, ace— a most straight and royal flush.
And so he had two working hands; one with five fingers and one with
fifty-two young girls who couldn't, and wouldn't, say no. ♠

This passage is seemingly unrelated to the instruction manuals
that weigh down poker players' bookshelves. Foer's piece has nothing to do with improving as a poker player or mastering advanced
no-limit hold 'em. But it is not unrelated to common poker themes.
Like a talented poker player, Foer's grandpa uses cards to demonstrate a manly skill (sex rather than poker). His mastery of these
cards allows him to win something from others (sex rather than
money). And I imagine he has to bluff a bit as well; it's unlikely he
told the fifty-second virgin about the previous fifty-one. Most
important, he taps into the wealth of lore, imagery, and symbolism
that even the most pragmatic gambler acknowledges. The game is
about winning and losing. But it is also about engaging in a manly

activity that feeds a (very literary) fantasy that each player is an heir to the legacy of poker coolness. That is why we read book after book to be more like the unread cowboys and riverboat gamblers and gangsters that long ago defined poker "cool." And that is why, win or lose, the fantasy keeps us coming back.

POKER FOR BASTARDS

by Dan Kelly

"Poker is merciless."

"Poker is a game of money and deception. The consequences
are always deserved. The penalties go to the weak—
the rewards go to the strong. The loser dissipates his time
and money. The winner earns satisfaction and money. . . . "

"Poker is sheer justice."

—From *Poker: A Guaranteed Income for Life by Using
the Advanced Concepts of Poker* (1968)

F OR PUREST MACHIAVELLIAN GLEE, few poker instruction
manuals match Frank R. Wallace's *Poker: A Guaranteed Income
for Life by Using the Advanced Concepts of Poker*. The book seems
innocuous enough. On the cover, five men play an intimate yet
intense game in a dark room—cigarette smoke and body heat fairly
rise off the cover. Four of the men, with mouths downturned, glower
at the center man, a wry fellow raking a mini-Matterhorn of chips
to his chest. The book invites us to join the cover game, though why
we would want to during a blood-drenched rout is not made clear.
Ah! But take heart, my friend. For with the Advanced Concepts, you
can turn even this table's bitter odds to your favor—and all it costs

is your immortal soul. Well, perhaps not in so many words, but darn close to it. Using the Advanced Concepts, proclaims the hyperbole, you can earn upward of "$150,000 a year . . . even more, much more. . . . " Sounds tasty, until you read on and discover how to turn a game with your buddies into a snarling psychological hellpit.

> . . . the poker player armed with the Advanced Concepts of Poker . . . knows how to control and manipulate the minds of players. He knows how to lure players into following their emotions, into losing control of themselves, into disorienting their psyches . . . even into destroying themselves.

The Advanced Concepts are ably illustrated by a game that could be going on in any basement, rec room, or garage. Our Advanced Concepts sensei is a fellow named John Finn, a gregarious social worker who believes in good clean fun and a friendly game of poker.

(Dramatic pause)

Or so his fellow players think.

In truth, in this Monday-night game and others, John Finn employs the Advanced Concepts to bilk his cronies out of thousands of dollars. Perhaps "milk" is the more apt verb. In this game, Finn is Farmer Brown, while his opponents are money moo-cows, their tumescent teats at the ready.

Finn's fellow players are straight out of summer stock. There's Sid, the garrulous and pudgy paving contractor, fidgety Ted Fehr, the gambling-addicted restaurateur, crotchety Professor Quintin Merck, the effete beret-wearing intellectual, and Scotty Nichols, a general-purpose shlemiel of no discernible personality. Gazing around the table at his prime Guernseys, John assays his competition with the compassion innate to social workers:

"'They're all valuable to me,' John Finn tells himself as his dark eyes draw into slits."

While the Advanced Concepts take 300-plus pages to fully manifest themselves, they are easily summarized in a few simple lessons.

As with *The Prince*, the omission of moral quandaries always distills instruction to its most effective essence. As a bonus, when employing the book one can always claim later that one was only following orders.

Lesson 1: Spy on Your Friends

Like other poker manuals, *Poker: A Guaranteed Income for Life by Using the Advanced Concepts of Poker* shows the interrelationship of odds for cards drawn versus bets placed, chock-a-blocking several pages with computational trellises. Unlike most manuals, this one declares interesting but negligible:

> If you are not mathematically inclined and do not understand this or other formulas and ratios presented in this chapter, do not worry. Just skip over the formulas and read on. For these formulas are not necessary to understand and utilize the concepts identified in this book.

Yep, ignore those daunting figures, chum. Game theory pales beside the penis-scissoring mindfucks offered here. Who needs to know the odds of drawing three queens when your opponents are but puny earthlings who believe in mystical notions like luck and sympathy?

To begin your descent into poker bastardy, invest in a little black notebook. One-man COINTELPRO John Finn creepily maintains precise records on each man's game and psychological hot buttons. For comparison purposes, note that the Advanced Concepts player is advised not to "swear or display feelings," and to "consume neither food nor beverage" during games. Finn is a poker android in these respects, also taking care to nap, bathe, foreswear demon rum before games, and otherwise keep himself samurai-sword sharp.

His opponents do not. Besides being unwashed and unshorn, Sid, Ted, Quintin, and Scotty all but weep blood on bad draws and hum Handel's *Messiah* when they fill a flush. As you read on, the other players reveal themselves to carry mental baggage the size of steamer trunks. Finn notes that Quintin is "[f]airly stable and objective," though "when insulted or humiliated" his play "disintegrates." In another case, Ted Fehr generally "wants to punish himself," and "[d]eteriorates easily into a desperate condition." Such a pack of twitching, neurotic sweatmonsters are the others that you wonder why Finn needs his *Book of Shadows* at all.

Lesson Two: Wrong Is Right

Dismiss traditional notions of morality with the Advanced Concepts. A falsehood is only improper when it serves you no benefit.

> Lying is a key tool of strategy. . . . With careful lying and calculated deceit, John Finn builds his image as a kindhearted, loose player who is an asset to the game.

During one game, the nigh-retarded Ted antes up $25 too much. Finn and Quintin see it, but say nothing. The hand proceeds apace, and after Finn snows Ted about drawing one card in the first round, Ted foolishly folds. As John shovels in his winnings, Ted picks up Finn's cards, looks at them, and shrieks: "'What! You play a four-flush pat to win a three-hundred-dollar pot?' John smiles and nods. Ted slumps in his chair.

"Our boy peels off twenty-five bucks and flips it to Ted.

"'What's this for?' Ted asks.

"'Your last bet,' John says. 'I don't feel right about taking it.'

"'Merciful guy.' Ted smiles. Then, counting the money, he continues, 'You might win all my money, but you're still a gentleman.'

"'That's no gift,' Quintin Merck mumbles, 'Ted put . . .'

"'Whose deal?' John interrupts. . . . So besides winning a $300 pot, [John] did a lot of favorable image-building. . . . "

Watching for flashed cards is another shady skill, ably demonstrated by Finn on Mike, a myopic newcomer:

John studies Mike's face very closely. Actually he is not looking at his face, but is watching the reflection in his eyeglasses. When Mike opens his hand, John sees the scattered dots of low cards plus the massive design of a picture card reflecting in the glasses. (. . . Occasionally a crucial card can even be identified in a player's bare eyeball.)

"Good players" remove themselves from "emotional situations," even revealing cheaters—with one predictable exception.

"The good player will . . . study an emotional situation in order to exploit it. He intervenes only in those situations that could cost him money."

One night the friendly game turns into an execration volcano. Ongoing rivals Sid and Quintin exchange bitter insults, coming close to fisticuffs. This summons Finn's characteristic empathy.

Since their bickering hurts their poker playing, John increases his winnings from the upset men. . . . But their animosity increases each week and John begins to worry. Blows are nearly exchanged when Quintin threatens to expose Sid's payola on city-paving contracts. Sid threatens to sue him for slander and then calls him a queer. Squinting his green eyes, Quintin cracks the edge of his hand on the table and threatens Sid with a karate blow. Sid vibrates his big fist close to Quintin's nose, calls him a queer again, and then storms out of the house while shouting that either he or Quintin must quit the game.

Finn plays goodwill ambassador, for fear of losing his prime patsy. Quietly, privately, John reminds the professor—the only other accomplished player, and the only one who can see the horns jutting from Finn's head—that Sid's submoronic playing allows them both to hang from him like blood-engorged ticks. Outraged, but not enough to develop a sense of ethics, Quintin agrees to apologize and continue to bleed Sid white. The hatchet is buried in Sid's back and Finn retains his status as a swell guy.

Lesson Three: Cloud Mens' Minds So They Cannot See You

In this section, Machiavelli is replaced by Svengali, though the book's hypnosis techniques seem as effective as a swinging gold pocket watch. Staring down your opponents or repeating subaudible chants (fold-fold-fold, raise-raise-raise) are suggested. If these ninja mind-spells fail to stupefy your opponent into bird-brained plays, molest the kitty.

> Scotty groans. Looking at the huge pot, he sees John's finger slowly stirring the pile of money—stirring slowly and smoothly. Ten- and twenty-dollar bills are moving in circles. Scotty's floating brown eyes start rotating with the money. His chubby hand slowly picks up a $100 bill. He calls the bet. Scotty tries to smile as John pulls in the pot. . . .

Even if this technique works on microcephalic Scotty, one wonders why Sid, Quintin, and Ted don't bother to ask John what the hell he's doing.

Elsewhere, Finn likes to prep rooms with distraction time-bombs. Mind-dulling liquor is served. TVs and radios blare. Newspapers showing the day's race results are placed near off-track-betting Ted. Employing the mesmerizing power of hooters, Finn even tosses porn hither and yon.

Lesson Four: Exploit Human Weakness

In Advanced Concept poker playing, the reptile brain is not sacrosanct. Chapter seventeen, "Exploitation," shows how to take advantage of the id with various black-bag tricks. In one instance, when Sid is injured and housebound, Finn brings the game to him. Knowing cheapskate Sid's cupboard is always bare, Finn visits a deli aforehand. The game sallies on, and at 3:00 A.M., Scotty's tummy rumbles angrily, sending him stumbling to Sid's kitchen to find naught but corn flakes. Seven-card stud is played, and John, wanting all to call, takes out his secret weapon . . . a hoagie!

> John lays the elongated sandwich across the pot. "The winners split it," he declares. . . . Scotty's face is sweating, and his stomach is growling.
>
> With eyes fixed on the sandwich, everyone calls the first bet. John aggressively bets his strong hand. Many players keep calling. The final bets are large. Scotty keeps calling with a poor hand. "Should fold," he says, catching his breath. "But that sub . . . yum" The red-faced man spends over $100 on calls. Three other players also call as their eyes remain fixed on the sandwich. The pot is the largest of the night—over $700. John wins both high and low with an ace-high full house and a six-five low. He also wins back the sandwich, which he later used to build another pot.

Incidentally, the above is a common POW/concentration-camp interrogation technique.

Our man John isn't always so parsimonious. Sometimes he provides sandwiches galore, stacked with cold cuts and slathered with extra mustard—all the better to have his unwitting opponents mark the cards with their sticky fingers.

Lesson Five: Play Against the Mentally Ill

Finn's treatment of the compulsive gambler Ted is a particularly troubling aspect of the Advanced Concepts. Rather than suggesting counseling, Finn instead jots down in his notebook:

> Ted Fehr
> Suicidal. Easy. Big loser.

Another game, and Finn is a card short of a flush. He bluffs, tossing fifty bucks into the pot to cast an anti-betting whammy on the
others. Everyone folds except lucky Ted, who holds two pair. He considers folding, but, soaring on a gambler's high, he stays in the game.
It's obvious to Finn that Ted is about to call. Can't have that, he
thinks. Knowing that superstitious Ted has—lord knows why—a
penny phobia, Finn the Bastard secretly slips a Lincoln head into a
corner of Ted's stack of cash. Grinning Ted decides to call. He grabs
a fistful of greenbacks, and . . . Horrors!

> "What!" His grin fades as the penny tumbles from the money. "No
> wonder I'm losing!" he yells while picking up the coin and throwing
> it across the room. As the penny bounces off the wall and rolls around
> the floor, Ted folds his hand and says, "At least that penny made me
> fold. I saved fifty bucks. . . . " His voice fades when John shows his
> winning hand . . . a four flush. Ted's eyes water. His superstition cost
> him a $200 pot.

Gradually, after tapping him like a maple tree for years, John sees
that Ted is drying up. Ted brings only a hundred bucks to the game,
desperately borrowing from the other players before the game is
halfway over. After giving Ted meager loans as it served his purposes,
Finn nixes further handouts and advises Ted to write checks. "Got
to have money to make money," he opines; a mantra Ted repeats with
enervated passion as he strips off a check. The next week, Ted does
well with the ponies and brings a grand to the game. You know what
happens.

> The excess cash clouds [Ted's] sense of value for money—he tries to
> overpower everyone. His overpowering play is an exhibition of wild,
> reckless poker. By two in the morning, Ted is writing a check; John
> Finn is a very big winner.

Avuncular Finn doesn't immediately abandon Ted. Like whispered sweet nothings in the ear, après-game heart-to-hearts keep a loser lubricated.

> The good player raises the morale of losers whenever possible. Sympathy and understanding properly offered can keep losers in the game indefinitely—or until they are bankrupt. . . .

In a chapter on gracefully leaving a game early (so that even if you've Hoovered your opponents' wallets, there are no hard feelings), we see Finn toss a reeducated Ted to the hyenas. After twenty-two hours of playing, John assiduously avoids the games that clean out Ted, who is on his restaurant's second mortgage. When Finn at last slithers out, his pockets bulge with cash and not a single IOU from now-catatonic, check-writing Ted. Soon, Sid and Scotty are tapped out, and when mean old Professor Merck won't cash his checks, Ted cracks like an ice rink in spring.

> . . . the freckle-faced man sits in a stupor and stares blankly at him with his mouth open. After a moment of eerie silence, Quintin stands up and says, "I'm going home." After another moment of silence, Sid and Scotty stand up to leave.
>
> "No, you can't leave!" Ted suddenly screams, rising from his chair. The players start rushing toward the door. "You took all my money! Please don't quit! I'm due for a comeback! I gotta win my mortgage money back! . . . I gotta!"

Ted sinks back into his chair with his arms falling to his side as everyone runs out the door. Continuing down the hallway, the players hear him calling out, "Please, give me a break . . . give me a break like John always does . . . like my friend John!"

(Fade to black.)

Atlas Bid

The major enemy of poker players is their rationalization for their failure to think. . . . Many poor players evade thinking by letting their
minds sink into irrational fogs. Their belief in luck short-circuits their
minds by excusing them from their responsibility to think. Belief in
luck is a great mystical rationalization for the refusal to think.

—From *Poker: A Guaranteed Income for Life by Using the
Advanced Concepts of Poker*

Sound familiar? If so, it's likely you carried around a copy of *Atlas
Shrugged* or *The Fountainhead* in your sophomore year. These
books probably likewise occupy space on Frank R. Wallace's book-
shelf, or they would if Frank R. Wallace existed. According to this
writer's sources, Mr. Wallace's real name is Dr. Wallace Ward: ex-
DuPont research scientist, ex-pro poker player, and founder of Neo-
Tech, a new-agey self-help program with shallow roots in Ayn Rand's
objectivist philosophy. Written in 1968, *Poker: A Guaranteed Income
for Life by Using the Advanced Concepts of Poker* was a Neo-Tech
harbinger, though Neo-Tech's ideas go well beyond the poker table,
and in some cases, beyond belief.

Wallace started the I/O Publishing Company (I/O standing for
individualism and objectivism) back in the early 1970s to sell his
Advanced Concepts to poker players worldwide. Perhaps sensing
that more money could be made by fighting rather than fostering
cardsharps, I/O Publishing's Neo-Tech publications provided personal improvement lessons with a more benign if bizarre bent.

Neo-Tech thought is far too extensive and fraught with hooey to
adequately portray here. Encapsulated, Dr. Ward drew life lessons
from his poker-playing days, during which he became aware of nefarious individuals he dubbed Neocheaters, those who "1. Promote a
myth" (e.g., "John Finn is my friend!"), in order to, "2. Gain
unearned values from those who accept the myth" (e.g., "John Finn

has taken all my money, yet he is still my friend!"). A poker player's use of the Advanced Concepts, claimed Neo-Tech, was analogous to the nefarious practices of Neocheaters in organized religion, the government, and the business world. Through Neocheating, so the story goes, "value destroyers" in these institutions kept our sheep-like selves in line while picking our pockets.

Still, don't think it would be easy to stop the Neocheaters. They were an Orwellian force, not only in poker but also in the rest of the universe.

> Neocheating is invisible. How can it be stopped? The Neocheater is
> impossible to catch in the act and hard to get rid of. In fact, all hon-
> est players unaware of Neocheating are in financial danger. The
> Neocheater is the most dangerous threat to ever invade the card tables.

Fear not, because Neo-Tech kills Neocheaters dead. Through "total integrated honesty" you could "collapse Neocheaters' personal mysticism" and reap untold benefits when you broke their hold on you. Yeah. Something like that.

While some "true" objectivists (a real cuddly bunch themselves) agree that Ward's *The Neo-Tech Discovery* closely follows Randian thought, Ward's later introduction of Zonpower lost them. Described as a cosmically powerful state we all experienced in early childhood, but have since forgotten how to use, Zonpower could make you wealthier, richer, sexier, and eventually immortal. Zonpower apparently also addled the brains of Neo-Tech's writers. "Zonpower lets you become GOD even without a computer," one perplexing piece of copy promises. " . . . Today, one can finally become free of the life-destroying humanoids infesting planet Earth." "Zonpower offers everyone the key to vanish this anticivilization beset with parasitical elites," offers another. Such gobbledygook is standard. The realpolitik of the Advanced Concepts manual possesses an unusual clarity not found in the labyrinthine prose of Ward's later books.

On the face of it, however, all Neo-Tech seemed to do was increase its users' ability to write checks to I/O Publishing and rambling testimonials on how Zonpower helped them claw their way to the middle. Arguably, Neo-Tech's methods worked—though largely for Dr. Ward and his company. The program, in its mid-'80s heyday, sold befuddling, dictionary-sized neo-Tech books at $90 and up.

Striving to keep the Neocheaters in check, Wallace didn't reckon he needed to watch the feds too. In 1986 the IRS caught a tip that the doctor was hoarding untaxed cash and gold. The feds swooped down on Neo-Tech, seized its assets, and locked Wallace up for a few years, giving him time to hammer out *The Neo-Tech Discovery*, an elucidation of the program's core philosophies, such as they were. The federal raid also struck the Neo-Technicians a little goofy: Neo-Tech's publications suddenly pulsated with chest-thumping "nothing can stop Neo-Tech!" rants and peculiar propagandistic images of Neo-Technicians ready to courageously catch bullets in their Zon-powered chests.

Neo-Tech continued to publish through the '90s, deciding in 1996 to "conquer the Internet." Its entire back catalog now rests at www.neo-tech.com—an impressive feat considering the raw amount of verbiage involved. Amoral poker players may enjoy the full text of the Advanced Concepts manual at www.neo-tech.com/poker. Pull up a chair, but consider whether you really want to be dealt in.

POKER ON TELEVISION

by Gentleman John Battles

Though the hundreds of channels available today have made it possible to regularly watch pros duke it out in televised poker tournaments, those shows are usually about as interesting as watching paint dry (and far less colorful). Real-life poker may be fun to play, but (with the exception of the game show Card Sharks, *and its naughty cable offspring,* Strip Poker*) it ain't too fun to watch in couch potato mode. True poker entertainment on the boob tube can be found by watching our fave fictional characters playing the game. When the gangs from* The Odd Couple, Taxi, *or* The Bernie Mac Show *ante up, the fun starts flying. And the drama of poker lends itself to action shows as well, as proven on* Maverick, Have Gun Will Travel, *and the poker-obsessed* Star Trek: The Next Generation. *The King of Card Games has made guest appearances on* I Love Lucy, The Dick Van Dyke Show, Friends, The Simpsons, *and countless other programs. On the following pages Gentleman John Battles, himself a real "card," reveals his favorite TV poker moments. Pull up your TV tray and enjoy:*

All in the Family: "Archie the Babysitter."
(Original airdate: January 12, 1976)

Lovable bigot Archie Bunker gets stuck watching his three-week-old grandson, Joey, on the same night he planned to host the big poker game with the boys from the loading dock (including, surprisingly, a young, hip-looking black guy). Undaunted, Archie decides to carry on with his poker game *and* babysit little Joey at the same time. Not surprisingly, things go awry. Joey starts crying, and Archie looks him over as though he was trying to find an on/off switch. His friends, eager to resume their card game, try to assist him. When someone suggests that the baby may need a diaper change, the doo-doo jokes abound (and the censors were aghast—not about the toilet humor, but about the baby's frontal nudity . . . another *All in the Family* first!). Soon, however, Archie's once (literally) poker-faced cronies begin to lose interest in their game and get mushy bonding with the baby. They forsake the poker chips to sing a manly lullaby. And Archie never does learn how to change a diaper. (Offensive poker addendum: On perhaps the most classic *All in the Family* episode, "Sammy's Visit" [February 19, 1972], Archie refers to Sammy Davis, Jr., as "the *ace* of spades.")

Sanford and Son: "The Card Sharps."
(Original airdate: October 27, 1972)

Lovable junkman Fred Sanford's son, Lamont, meets up with a group of con men whose pimpin' threads make Lamont's buddy, Rollo, look like a banker. Lamont thinks nothing of their sleazy attire and accepts their challenge to "a friendly game of poker." Fred smells a rat (in purple alligator shoes!), and tries to warn Lamont, but his indignant son shines him on. It seems Lamont can't lose, even against seasoned players; he somehow manages to beat them at every hand. By this time, the "big dumb dummy" should have known he was flying right into their web. But persistent warnings from Fred (once a poker-man before he promised his late wife Elizabeth that he'd never play again) only make Lamont more determined to carry on with the game. When he agrees to give his opponents a chance to win their money back, Lamont gets fleeced. Fred discovers that the cards were marked, and can only be read with sunglasses, which, incidentally, the other guys have been wearing the whole time (Lamont, of course, suspects nothing). Fred then (with apologies to Elizabeth) ropes the players into one last game by acting like a clueless pigeon. His adversaries laugh at him, but Fred has the last laugh. As the show ends Sanford is counting *all* their money while wearing *all* their fly clothes (several furs and coats layered one upon another), and for good measure he checks the time . . . on an arm weighed down with a half-dozen watches.

The Sopranos: "The Happy Wanderer."
(Original airdate: February 20, 2000)

Lovable mobster Tony Soprano decides to bring back an old tradition introduced to him by his father and his Uncle Junior: "The Executive Game," a marathon poker session where the sky's the limit. Among the esteemed players, Frank Sinatra, Jr., (as himself) steals the show, despite a relatively short time on screen. The game is interrupted early on when Davie Scatino, a high school buddy of Tony's, stops by. Impressed by Sinatra's presence, Davie tells Tony, "Wow, this *is* an executive game . . . what do you think?" Tony replies that he can see the resemblance (between Sinatras Jr. and Sr.). "No, I mean, what do you think about (letting me play in) the game?" He then begs his way into a seat at the table, despite Tony's warnings that the stakes are too high for a guy who runs a sporting-goods shop. Tony even fronts Davie an exponentially growing bankroll (as we are reminded that "a box a ziti" is $1,000). Later Paulie Walnuts calls Frankie the "Chairboy of the Board" and tells him to "read your fucking cards!" (Sinatra on Paulie: "Don't be scared of Paulie. . . . He's not really a nasty fuck. He's an *incredibly* nasty fuck.") Meanwhile, two green kids who wish to be "made" some day serve the food and drinks, and incur the wrath of Silvio Dante for trying to clean up some cheese he spilled on the carpet. Frank Jr. later tips one of the kids, who replies, "Thank you, Mr. Sinatra, Jr., . . . sir!" The Executive Game goes south with the arrival of weasely Richie, who disrespects the game by attempting to take Davie outside to "sort him out" (Davie owes Richie several grand in poker debts). Davie, meanwhile, finds himself in the hole to Tony to the tune of forty-five boxes of ziti (which will eventually be collected, Soprano-style). From Tony's standpoint (drama aside), the game proves successful, raking in about 80 Gs for him and his boys. Sil, always there with the last word, is quick to point out that a good piece of that was his.

The Phil Silvers Show: "New Recruits."
(Original airdate: September 20, 1955)

Lovable con man and compulsive gambler Sgt. Bilko (Silvers) often made poker a centerpiece of one of the greatest sitcoms ever. In the premiere episode, sly Bilko loses for the first time ever and a deep depression sets in (though not deep enough to keep him from trying to scrape together a bankroll for next week's game). The chaplain pays Bilko a visit, and, stunned to learn that he has lost a card game, decides to take advantage of Bilko's vulnerability. He arranges for Bilko's platoon to be transferred and replaced with a fleet of remarkably naive rookies. One can almost see dollar signs in Bilko's eyes and hear the cash register ringing in his head as he unleashes an evil grin and says, "New blood!" He has fallen right into the chaplain's trap. The new recruits are led by a killjoy PFC who thwarts Bilko's efforts to encourage his new boys to do anything that involves being lax in their duties or (worst of all!) parting with the money they

brought from home (which Bilko covets as a bankroll for his weekend game). Imagine Bilko's surprise when the same PFC later
implores the sergeant to hold *all* their money until their first pay
period one month later. It turns out that the chaplain told the PFC
to trust Sgt. Bilko with the money, as he was the one man worthy of
such faith. To the surprise of all, this trust creates something resem-
bling a conscience in Bilko. Saturday rolls around, and Bilko's two
henchmen, played with the usual zest by Harvey Lembeck (who can
also be seen as Eric Von Zipper in the Frankie-and-Annette beach
movies) and Allan Melvin (Sam the butcher on *The Brady Bunch*,
Barney Heffner on *All in the Family*, and various Mayberry
characters . . . where's his lifetime achievement award?) tell the Sarge
he's got to get into the game, it's a sure thing. To add insult to injury,
Bilko draws cards in his room to ease the tension, and comes up aces
every time! Does he finally crack? You'd think so, but the next day
the chaplain is seen congratulating Bilko, content in the knowledge
that the little ploy worked a miracle. The next evening, Barbella and
Henshaw (Lembeck and Melvin) are seen standing armed watch over
the PFC, sleeping with the money in his hand, while Bilko snoozes
cheerfully, with (ulp!) a clear conscience. Not to worry, though: Bilko
has a productive career of fleecing ahead of him. On one of Bilko's
many other poker campaigns, he and the boys at the motor pool fall
prey to Poker Interruptus. Bilko is bilkin' 'em when the TV starts to
garner attention with a political broadcast. A congressman dares to
suggest that enlisted men were living large, eating the finest foods
and drinking the best imported champagnes, to which the Sarge
retorts, "This is domestic if I've ever tasted it!" The congressman
goes on to accuse the army of spending federal funds to support
gambling and drinking vices. "That's a lie!" Bilko says. "We stole
that stuff from the officer's club!" Eventually, Sgt. Bilko and his boys
resume their card game, but not without a short lecture from a
player, who agrees with the congressman and alerts the other to the

fact that a sergeant makes over $260 a month (which I guess was a lot of money back then). Bilko sees and raises the accusation by turning up all aces and walking away with the pot.

Ghoulardi
(circa early 1960s)

Lovable TV horror-movie host, Ghoulardi (real name Ernie Anderson, also known as Tim Conway's stand-up partner, the voice of ABC in the 1970s, and the father of *Boogie Nights* director Paul Thomas Anderson), owns one of my favorite TV poker moments, which occurred live on local Cleveland televison in the early 1960s. An ad-libbing Ghoulardi, apparently at a loss for enough material to fill his time slot, addressed his (mostly teen and preteen) audience by asking them, "You wanna know how to play poker? You get a girl, and then you poke 'er!" Goulardi's local popularity was so great that he wasn't concerned about the anger of the censors, parents, and community leaders (nor was he concerned about corrupting the joyful kids who actually got it). In one of many games of chance, Ghoulardi won yet again.

LI'L ART'S POKER PARTY

AN INTERVIEW WITH ART FEIN

by Jake Austen

In January 1984 record collector Art Fein gathered his buddies at an L.A. public-access TV studio and launched what would become one of the longest-running, most legendary programs in cable access's humble history. Li'l Art's Poker Party *took the absurdity, goofiness, and convoluted conversations of a neigh- borhood poker game and televised it to Tinseltown. "Each show would begin with a poker hand being dealt (to four sort-of friends) and slowly evolve into a series of conversations/argu- ments on all sorts of topical b.s.," Poker Partyer Richard Meltzer recalls. "At its best, it was one of the more existentially genuine whatsems in the annals of TV (honest). At its worst, it was ersatz TV-hokum like anything else." Though the actual card games were phased out of the show after a few years, the ersatz talk show, renamed* Art Fein's Poker Party *in 1989, is still going strong. Guests over the years have included Dwight Yoakam, George Wendt, Screamin' Jay Hawkins, Keith Morris of Black Flag, Johnny Ray, Ike Turner, Eric Burdon, and hundreds more. Here Mr. Fein explains the evolution of the show that for almost*

two decades has given Los Angelenos an alternative to the Friday evening news.

Jake Austen: How was *Li'l Art's Poker Party* born?

Art Fein: My friends and I used to talk about music when we played poker in my kitchen. Nobody could play poker very well and it was just funny. I'd heard about this thing called public-access television, and I'd seen various amateurs on TV doing senseless things, and I thought I could do it, too.

JA: Who were some of the people who used to play at your house?

AF: Rock journalists Richard Meltzer, Gene Sculatti, Tod Everett. The writer Nick Tosches came to a couple of the games. Keith Joe Dick, the Rockabilly Romeo. Just writers and music people. It would always be something we looked forward to.

JA: You said you weren't good at poker. What do you mean by that?

AF: I was good at poker, but the others were not. They just came to pass the time, but a lot of them wanted to know how to play poker. We played for nickels; it was just silly. It was actually just men pretending to be men. Remember, these guy didn't know what they were doing, so we kept it at a nickel ante, which makes it very hard to bluff.

JA: So how did your kitchen game evolve into playing on TV?

AF: At the time we were having fun playing poker, and not really playing poker, and it struck me that we should do this on television. I started getting cable, and I noticed the type of people that were on public access. I contacted the station, and they asked me to submit a script, a rundown of how the show would go. So I wrote down a bunch of conversations that were virtually true. My script was just our actual poker talk.

JA: Describe the early shows.

AF: We had huge theatrical cards behind us on the wall—a king, a queen, a jack, and an ace. That was the visual look of the show. We'd actually play cards, but it was surreal, senseless. We'd play silly games; we'd play three-card Indian . . .

JA: You would just hold three cards face out on your foreheads?

AF: Yeah. That would heighten the drama for the people watching at home.

JA: What other games would you play?

AF: Meltzer would usually name games after people he didn't like. "This is three-card Hilburn, because it doesn't make any sense." Robert Hilburn is the rock critic at the *L.A. Times*. It didn't matter. Since we had no business and no experience doing a television talk show, the poker was there as something to fall back on. When we ran out of things to say we'd say, "Well. I think it's your bet."

JA: So you would continuously be playing a game, but with long breaks between the action where you would talk about various topics . . .

AF: Exactly. And we had poker chips.

JA: So no cash money was passing hands, but did you have to settle up your losses at the end of the game?

AF: No, it was like the show *Whose Line Is It Anyway?*, where they give away "points." At the end they say the show has a million points and none of them matter. We played for "points." Also, I would like to mention one thing that really ticked me off. Two years after *Li'l Art's Poker Party* started, a poker show came out of Chicago with a bunch of sports guys with cigars sitting around a table playing poker while they discussed sports topics.

JA: *The Sportswriters on TV?*

AF: Yes. I don't think it was coincidental.

JA: Why did you phase the poker out of the show?

AF: We smoked cigars on the set while we played poker, and after a couple of years the people who used the studio after us, some kind of flower show, they really didn't dig the cigar smoke. Lots of people objected to the smell. They had us put out the cigars and that kind of put out the poker. But a lot of people enjoy the fact that it's still called a poker party even though there's no poker.

JA: Do you still play poker?

AF: No, in the '80s I got involved with some newspaper people who had a poker game. But when there's a clique and they have special rules that they all know and you don't, you lose track because you're not as familiar with the house rules. I was losing pretty badly at a time when I couldn't afford it, and they weren't taking any mercy on me.

JA: Do you think you will continue to do the show indefinitely?

AF: Oh, yeah. As I explained to my wife, some people drink or do drugs. I have the *Poker Party*.

POKER IN COMEDY

by Jake Austen

POKER HAS BEEN a favorite subject of American humorists from Mark Twain ("There are few things that are so unpardonably neglected in our country as poker") to Steven Wright ("I stayed up all night playing poker with tarot cards. I got a full house and four people died"), and cards and comedy have intersected in many funny ways over the 170 years or so since America embraced the pasteboards. W. C. Fields's trademark was his poker-playing slickster persona (from his 1940 film *My Little Chickadee*: "Is this a game of chance?" "Not the way I play it, no."). Gabe Kaplan (best known for his sitcom *Welcome Back, Kotter*) retired from stand-up to become a successful professional poker player. One of David Letterman's comedy writers, Jill A. Davis, wrote the best-selling novel *Girls' Poker Night*. And Bernie Mac, one of the "Kings of Comedy," makes poker a part of his live act, his movie appearances, and his television show.

And while most poker one-liners are about as sophisticated as "liquor in the front, poker in the rear," simple jokes aren't the heart of great comedy. Just as a good night of poker comes not from a single hand, but from a long night of deals, the best comedy is about building a narrative. Though my favorite poker comedy recordings are somewhat obscure, they are worth seeking out, as listening to these is as fun as successfully drawing to an inside straight.

◆

Christine Nelson was a comedienne best known as the female voice on "Sarah Jackman," a standout track from Allen Sherman's best-selling comedy LP *My Son the Folk Singer* (Warner Brothers, 1962). Sung to the tune of "*Frère Jacques*," the song has Nelson (as the Jewess Jackman) kibitzing about her family on the telephone. Several years later Nelson revisited the Jackman character in an unjustly obscure comedy concept-album called *Didja Come to Play Cards or to Talk?* (Reprise, 1966), a record about Jackman and her girlfriends' Tuesday night poker game (Bela, Frida, Zelda, Rosie, and Sadie round out her six).

The track "Don't Leave the Table" demonstrates that this isn't just a poker record, it's a gender-specific poker record. During their card game Sarah looks forward to one of the other girls leaving her seat, allowing the crew to viciously slander and gossip about their "friend." The song ends with Jackman refusing to leave her seat even though her bathroom is flooded, her kitchen is on fire, and her kid is turning blue.

The next poker song is much more focused on card play, as a hand of poker is set to opera in "Pokeracci." Ruggiero Leoncavallo's opera *Pagliacci* has long been a favorite of funny folk, perhaps because of its clown theme, but more likely because of its memorable music. Back in an era when even snot-nosed kids were expected to have a measure of highbrow cultural literacy (in the 1950s *Mad* magazine regularly ran parodies of classic poetry, and cartoons featured zany takes on classical music), this opera was parodied by Homer and Jethro ("When we listen to Pal-yat-chee/We get itchy and scratchy . . ."), Ray Bolger on the *Colgate Comedy Hour*, and the great Sid Caesar. The tragic clown is still fodder for humor these days, making relatively recent appearances on the TV shows *Animaniacs* and *Seinfield*.

In "Pokeracci" the humor is mainly derived from hearing about a lowly poker hand, sung in operatic fashion by a nasal, ethnic voice. Though they don't rhyme and aren't particularly clever, imagine these opening lines sung in high dramatic fashion: "Wretched cards! I've never seen such garbage before! What did I do to deserve such rotten hands? Hey, wait a minute, I don't believe it! I've got two aces in the hole and they don't know! This pot is destined to be mine (*laughs maniacally*)."

By the time Sarah turns her pocket rockets into trips, Bela is showing a low pair and Frida just has queen high. As the opera comes to its crescendo, Sarah shows her hand ("*ridi Pagliacci . . .*" becomes "I have three aces . . .") only to be trumped by Bela's four sixes. But in a twist of fate, it turns out that Bela has six cards. Her hand is dead, and Sarah fulfills her destiny.

Side two opens with the title track, which revisits the theme of the overly chatty poker players ("We're the Tuesday-night poker-game crowd, we're prim and we're proper and proud! We seldom play more hands than three hands or four hands cause everyone's talking too loud"), but at least this time the serious poker player at the table is annoyed. The highlight is when Sarah tells Frida, who is worried about her ass looking fat in slacks, to "forget about *yours* and think of *our* pot."

The album then ends with the most universal of its poker songs, "Gripes," in which Nelson (in a nod to Sherman) parodies a dozen or so famous melodies by applying lyrics about her fellow players' annoying habits, such as, "I took the high hand and you took the low hand, but who gets the one chip remaining? I think that it's better that I give the chip to you or I'll never hear the end of your complaining."

This album balances very broad, corny one-liners and insult humor with the more challenging task of asking listeners to identify with poker-playing urban Jewish housewives. Perhaps the most mind-blowing concept of this concept album is that, if she's using her real name, it is very unlikely that Ms. *Christine* Nelson (unless her parents were an early sect of Jews for Jesus) was even Jewish.

◆

One artist whose Judaism cannot be challenged is Mickey Katz, the Yiddish Weird Al Yankovic. A strange hybrid recording artist, he was a clarinetist leading a hot progressive klezmer band and he was the corny comedian making Yiddish/English parody records of contemporary hits ("Don't Let the Schmaltz Get in Your Eyes," "Borscht Riders in the Sky"). Though recognized now as a twisted genius (Don Byron has paid tribute to him), Katz's recordings are rarely heard, which has left his great poker comedy routine to fall by the wayside.

Katz Pajamas (1959, Capitol) was an unusual album for Katz. Instead of an all-music LP, it was a children's album in which he told Yiddish-ified fairy tales in both song and spoken word. Poker does not poke its head into "Little Red Rosenberg" or "Bagel-Lox and the Tree Bears," but it is featured as the climax of the western tale "Fancy Herringer."

Fancy Herringer is a cowboy who heeded Horace Greenberg's directive and "vent Vest." A tough guy, handy with a pistol, "when this boy gave a *shiess* (shot) it was *kaddish* time at the ranch." Trouble starts when Katz Masterson moseys in and they engage in a high-stakes game of draw poker. "Everybody gathered around these two *ferbrennte* gamblers," and when they each bet their mezuzahs the crowd "knew that the game was absolutely strictly kosher." With much gelt and their mezuzahs on the table, Fancy shows five aces to Katz's five kings. The confused crowd finally realizes they were mistakenly playing with a pinochle deck!

There are a few things that are particularly interesting about this routine. Though it is less musically engaging than most Katz songs, the spoken nature of this record actually allows the jokes to come faster and funnier than in a rhyming tune. Also, to a contemporary audience it may seem odd that a cowboy story was considered to be of the same status as fairy tales when it came to kiddie fare. This is especially striking when you note that gambling and drinking (Fancy "could hold his schnapps" and says "*L'chayim*" with a glass of shlivovitz) was accepted as part of the lore. But I suppose that this entire album would be so confusing to your child that explaining the gambling references would be the least of your concerns.

♦

Katz's record is a good one, but it isn't my favorite poker comedy recording. The greatest poker comedy record—in fact, possibly the greatest poker record ever made—isn't technically a comedy record at all.

The African American art form of "toasting" is an oral tradition in which dramatic narratives (often featuring unlikely heroes) are dynamically performed by an orator. These folk poems were sparsely documented (either archived only by academics or introduced into popular culture in drastically altered form, such as the pop song "Stagger Lee") until 1970. In that year Rudy Ray Moore, a comedian and R&B singer since the 1950s, began releasing fairly traditional toasts as part of his comedy albums, "officially" associating toasting with stand-up comedy.

"Toasting relates to comedy because it has comedic overtones to it," Moore explains. "You can take certain forms of toasting and make hard comedy out of it. These toasts make people laugh, and anytime you can jerk a laugh out of a person it would be associated with comedy."

That logic is somewhat complicated by the fact that the same year Moore began releasing toast records as comedy, the Last Poets combined elements of toasting with radical black politics and modernist poetry to create a record as serious as Moore's records were comedic. Three years later Last Poet Alafia Pudim (later known as Jalal Nuriddin) released *Hustler's Convention* (United Artists, 1973) under the persona Lightnin' Rod.

The Lightnin' Rod album is an amazing recording. The entire thing is one epic toast about a young hustler named Sport and his ace-boom coon Spoon negotiating the underworld of drugs, fine bitches, and high-stakes gambling in one remarkable night. Featuring big-name funky musicians including Kool & the Gang, Buddy Miles, King Curtis, and Billy Preston, and with a more rhythmic, lyrical delivery than Moore's, this album should be allowed to determine its own fate. But there was no way a toast LP, released in the wake of Rudy Ray Moore's phenomenally influential *Dolemite*, could be totally removed from the realm of comedy. And more important, the boasts, hyperbole, and vulgarity of this story are (in addition to being exciting, scary, thrilling, and intimidating) very *funny*.

Though the story has the antiheroes gambling in a dice game, pool hall, and police shootout, it is at the poker table where this album reaches its artistic peak. In "Four Bitches Is What I Got" we are treated to perhaps the most dramatic game of poker ever documented on wax.

With amazing music by Kool & the Gang in the background, Sport and Spoon sit in on a very-high-stakes game and collude until one of them holds a hand that looks like a winner ("Spoon coughed back twice, letting me know he was nice").

They make raises until the bets are into the tens of thousands, and only the nervous hustler Spongey is left in the game, showing jacks. After a round of massive betting, both players draw two. Spoon signals to Sport that he made his four-of-a-kind, but Spongey opens with heavy betting. Spoon sees, and with $110,000 in the pot they reveal their holdings. "Spongey laid down his hand, saying, 'Four studs my man!,' and reached over to scoop up the pot. But Spoon stopped him cold, saying, 'It's about time you were told, four bitches is what I got!'"

Their night goes south from there, with a double cross and a brush with the law leaving Sport shot up and on death row. When he gets a retrial and hits the streets a dozen years later, the traditional toast form is broken, as Sport has seen the political way in prison and now prepares for the revolution, realizing that his hundred grand was chump change compared to The Man's crooked billions. But any opinion one would have about the end of the record has to take a back seat to the awe one feels after the stunning poker tale this album climaxes with. The rhythm of the game, the tension of the betting, and the revelation of the cards are all portrayed vividly in the song. While it may not be as funny as the Jewish poker records, and it may not be as metaphorical as country poker records, this recording is in many ways the audio document that best captures the magic of the game.

♦

A cult classic that heavily influenced hip hop, *Hustler's Convention* has been reissued at least twice on CD and is not impossible to find. I urge you to seek out this, as well as the harder-to-track-down Nelson and Katz records. I'd wager that if you get to experience these recordings firsthand, it will be very difficult for you to maintain a poker face.

"THE DARKTOWN POKER CLUB"

by Bert Williams

Introduction by Jake Austen

Illustration by Chris Ware

T HOUGH LITTLE-KNOWN TODAY, Bert Williams was one of the most popular entertainers of the early twentieth century. According to his audiences and colleagues, he was one of the all-time greatest American performers (W. C. Fields called him "the funniest man I ever saw"). Born in 1875 in the West Indies, Egbert Austin Williams moved to California at a young age and steered himself toward a career in minstrel shows, the most popular form of theater of the day. With humor based on African American stereotypes and presented in heavy, preposterous dialect, minstrel shows are today associated solely with racist white actors in "blackface" makeup. However, minstrel shows were also performed by black actors (like Williams) who, in keeping with minstrel conventions, often wore blackface makeup themselves.

While Williams wore the makeup (his light complexion was perhaps confusing to white audiences), it was the amazingly expressive face under the burnt cork that made him a star. Williams's talents as a physical comedian, humorist, and songwriter began, by the mid-

1890s, to earn him the reputation that would make him the Jackie Robinson of American theater. As a member of the comedy team Williams and Walker (with George Walker), he was part of the first black production on Broadway. He would also become the first African American to star in integrated vaudeville sketches, and after launching a solo career in the wake of Walker's departure (due to illness), he became the first black star of the Ziegfeld Follies.

Two of Williams's most famous routines involved poker. Perhaps the best documented example of Williams's genius occurs in the film *A Natural Born Gambler* (1916), in which he demonstrates his brilliant solo pantomime poker routine. With an invisible deck, Williams shuffles, deals the cards, betrays all theories of "poker face" by joyously reacting to his hand's contents, and then has his visage of elation morph into crushed defeat when his imaginary opponent reveals his holdings. His other noted poker routine, a highlight of *The Ziegfeld Follies of 1914*, is the song "The Darktown Poker Club," for which Williams was the lyricist.

The tune was based on a popular 1888 book by white author Henry Guy Carleton, son of a Civil War hero and himself a successful novelist, playwright, and journalist. *The Thompson Street Poker Club* and its 1889 sequel, *The Lectures Before the Thompson Street Poker Club*, were initially serialized in the early 1880s in the original *Life* magazine (a New York humor weekly), for which Carleton was associate editor. The series was a sensation due in part to the illustrations of E. W. Kemble, who later parlayed his knack for minstrel cartooning into his most famous work—illustrating *The Adventures of Huckleberry Finn*. More important, the series was successful because it relied on racist stereotypes and the absurd black dialect that was extremely popular in turn-of-the-century literature. The episodes consisted of moderately amusing card games between characters with names like Cyanide Whiffles and Thankful Smith. Here's a typical exchange between Mr. Smith and Tooter Williams:

"Ez my fre' Toots done open that jacker?"

"What yo' go do dat for, Brer Thankful? Dat's not the speret ob de Gospil."

"Is yo' goin' ter pray or poke?"

"I'se gwine ter poke. I'se gwine to see yo' rise."

What's most notable about Williams's adaptation of the concept is the shift in dialect. The transcription that follows, made from Williams's best-selling 1914 Columbia 78-rpm record of the song, demonstrates a dignity and humanity that Carleton's characters are lacking. While Williams's Bill Jackson (already a far more human sobriquet than "Cyanide Whiffles") speaks in dialect at times, he also demonstrates that he is *choosing* to speak "black English" for emphasis, not out of ignorance of proper English. He contrasts the fact that they will not play *according* to Hoyle with his declaration that they will play "accordin'" to him. On the first chorus Williams (as Jackson) enunciates the word "more," but as he brings it home in the closing reprise he emphasizes the black English pronunciation "mo'." Most important, Williams, as the story's black narrator, is himself an eloquent, dignified orator.

"The Darktown Poker Club" had a long musical life after its 1914 heyday. In the 1940s bandleader Phil Harris had a huge novelty hit with the song, and it became his signature for decades to come. It reemerged as a street-corner serenade in the early 1950s, when black doo wop groups such as the Ravens performed it live. It was even revived several years ago (with "Darktown" excised from the title) when Lonnie Donegan recorded a version for his would-be comeback album.

Williams's fame has not been as enduring. He died at age forty-seven in 1922 (his burial integrated a Masonic cemetery), and eighty years later his legacy seems as invisible as his pantomime poker opponents. However, what little documentation we have of Bert Williams and his comedy still holds up. *A Natural Born Gambler* is available on video, his image appears in Spike Lee's minstrel-themed

◆ *Natural Born Gambler* ◆

film *Bamboozled*, and his recordings can be located all over cyberspace. More important, he blazed a trail that allowed black comedians to change the face of American comedy.

The Darktown Poker Club
by Bert Williams

Bill Jackson was a poor old dub.
He joined the Darktown Poker Club,
Then cussed the day they told him that he could join.

His money seemed like it had wings:
If he held queens someone had kings.
Each night he would contribute *all* his coins.

So he says, "I think I'll play 'em tight tonight:
No bobtail flush will make me bite;
When I go in my hand'll be a peach."

Ha—So he'd go on in and lose his pile,
And he got kinda peevish after a while.
One night he got up and made a speech:

Said, "You see this brand new razor,
I had it sharpened just today.
Now I want to tell y'all some new rules to follow
Hereafter when *we* play.

"Keep your hands above the table when you're dealin' . . . please.
And I don't wanna catch no aces down between your knees.
Don't be makin' funny signs or tip your hand,
And I don't want to hear no kinda language that I don't understand.

"Stop dealin' from the bottom, cause it looks so rough.
  And remember that in poker five cards is . . . enough.
  When you bet, put up, cause I don't like it when you shy.
  And when you're broke get up and then come on back by and by.

"Pass the cards to me to shuffle every time before you deal,
  Then there's anything's wrong, well *I'll* see.
  We're not going to play this game no more according to Mr. Hoyle.
  Hereafter it's gon' be accordin' to *me*."

Now seated right there in the clan,
  There chanced to be a one-eyed man.
  Bill watched him from the corner of his eye.

The one-eyed man would deal and then
  It would cost Bill Jackson five or ten.
  Finally he got up with a sigh,

"Ahhh," he says, "I think that it 'tis a shame,
  But there's cheatin' going on in the game,
  And honestly, I . . . I don't wanna name the guy.

"But where I may not call his name,
  If I think I catch him cheatin' again,
  I'm gonna take my fist and close his other eye.

"Pass them cards to me to shuffle every time before you deal,
  Then there's anything's wrong, well *I'll* see.
  We ain't goin' to play this game no mo' according to Mr. Hoyle.
  Hereafter it's just accordin' to *me*."

poker and basketball

an interview with johnny "red" kerr

by Dave Hoekstra

JOHN "RED" KERR is an old hand at playing poker among basketball's jocks and kings. A Chicago Bulls broadcaster since 1973,
Kerr first played poker in 1952 when he was center for the University of Illinois basketball team that won the Big Ten championship
(and lost to St. John's in the Final Four).

Kerr won titles his first year of playing at each level—high school,
college, and the NBA with the 1955 Syracuse Nationals. "The worst
thing you can do in poker is to be second best," says Kerr, who grew
up the son of a Scottish bricklayer on the south side of Chicago. "If
you start to run into some things when you're gettin' cards, but you're
second best all the time, you're best to get out of the game. I always
liked the theory that if you didn't win the first pot, you couldn't win
them all."

Kerr has seen poker move from buses to trains to commercial air-
lines to private charters. "I remember the first time I won big," Kerr
says. "We took a slow bus ride from Champaign (home of the University of Illinois) some twenty-five miles down the road to Paxton. I won
$65 in a game. And that was like mint. After I got to $65, I asked someone if I could get it changed into singles. I thought I had a lot of money."

After college, the six-foot, ten-inch center went on to have a distinguished twelve-year NBA career with Syracuse, Philadelphia, and Baltimore. Kerr was a three-time NBA all-star. He was the first coach of the Chicago Bulls (1966–67).

As Bulls broadcaster, Kerr witnessed the notorious 1990s poker games led by Michael Jordan, Ron Harper, and Scottie Pippen. "I saw some very high-stakes card games," says Kerr, (who is no relation to squeaky-clean NBA guard Steve Kerr). "I wasn't involved in them, but I was on the plane with them."

I covered the 1990–91 NBA-champion Bulls for the *Chicago Sun-Times*. I never flew charter, but I heard how coaches warned younger players not to play poker with Jordan. The bald one, of course, would bet on anything. The most popular story on press row at the old Chicago Stadium centered on the M&M race on the center-court scoreboard. Animated red, green, and yellow M&Ms—about the size of poker chips—would race around a track. Before the game Jordan asked the scoreboard operator which chip was going to win that night. Later, during the game, when he took his accustomed seat near the fans at the end of the bench while resting, Jordan often bet a fan $5, offering one sure color against their two. He was a shark.

While Jordan got wound up about poker, Kerr used the game to wind down during his early NBA career. "We used to travel mostly by train," Kerr says. "We'd play in the sleeper car or we'd go in the club car. We'd play poker, draw poker, seven-card stud, and have a couple of beers until we got tired. You had to. You had six-foot, nine-inch and six-foot, ten-inch guys trying to get into a six-foot bunk. We played nickel-dime-quarter to pass the time. When [Syracuse] traded [guard] Dick Barnett to the Knicks, it cost me about $1,000 in nickel-dime."

Poker playing didn't affect Kerr's basketball play. He held the NBA consecutive-game record (844, 1954–65) before Randy Smith broke it in 1982–83 (with 906). Kerr is one of the select NBA players who totaled more than 10,000 points and 10,000 rebounds in his career.

Poker in the NBA took off with fancy travel. "You couldn't really play cards on a commercial airline flight," Kerr says. "Having other passengers on the plane, that was difficult. With the charters, it's easy to get together and have long card games. But now most of the guys watch DVDs. You don't see as many card games as you used to." As for Kerr, when he is on the road these days, he listens to his complete collection of Waylon Jennings CDs—including "Jack o' Diamonds," of course.

Intimate group dynamics are involved when non-casino poker meets the world of pro basketball. "Only four or five players would be involved," Kerr says. "It wasn't like going to someone's house to play poker. We were with the players every day. It's not like there was an outsider in the game."

Kerr says that the late, great Wilt Chamberlain was the best poker player he saw. The Stilt and Red were teammates along with Chet Walker and Hal Greer on the 1964–65 Philadelphia '76ers. "I played with Wilt a year and a half," Kerr says. "He didn't care about anything. He was fearless. He'd just bet and scare the hell out of you. He'd always bet big money, which the rest of us didn't have."

Kerr recalls that some players had superstitions: "Guys would say, 'Never cut green timber,'" Kerr says. "It was bad luck to cut the cards. Some guys liked to ante last to make sure everyone was in. We played games like 'Hitler's death' and 'between the sheets' (where two cards up—could be between an ace and a king—you'd bet [on] something in-between. If you tied or went over, you lost)."

Coaches were not invited to participate in NBA poker games. As a coach of the Bulls and, later, the Phoenix Suns, Kerr didn't mind that his players played poker. "I just didn't like to see them get into big games," he says. "I'd just tell them that I played a lot when I was a player and we never went over a dollar. I'd say to keep the pot low so nobody gets hurt."

Kerr is always smiling, which makes him a better poker player. He smiles and adds, "Without naming names, there was a Chicago sportswriter [not me] who covered us on the beat for many years that used to get in the card games. I thought that was kind of strange. You'd get in the card game, some guy would beat you in a hand, and then you would write about how poorly he played (basketball). But normally, poker is just a player's game."

Teaching Petey Poker by Heather McAdams

about the contributors

Ashley Adams has been playing poker since learning the game from his grandfather in 1962. He plays all over the world and has won tournaments in Las Vegas, Connecticut, and California. He is the author of the book, *Winning 7-Card Stud* (Kensington Press, 2003), and has regular columns in www.thepokerforum.com and in *Southwestern Poker Player Magazine*. By profession he is a union negotiator and an agent for broadcasters in New England. Most evenings, when he is home, you can find him playing poker online or posting as asha34 on the Internet poker discussion group Rec.Gambling.Poker.

Benjamin Austen is an editor at *Harper's* magazine. His writing has appeared in various newspapers and publications, including the *Philadelphia Inquirer* and the *Austin American-Statesman*.

Jake Austen edits *Roctober Comics and Music* magazine, the journal of popular music's dynamic obscurities, and (with his wife Jacqueline) produces the cable-access children's dance show *Chic-A-Go-Go*. His work has appeared in *The Cartoon Music Book* (A Cappella, 2002), *Nickelodeon Magazine*, *Playboy*, *Spice Capades: The Spice Girls Comic Book* (Fantagraphics, 1999), *Bogus Dead* (Jeroman,

2002), and *Bubblegum Music Is the Naked Truth* (Feral House, 2001).

Gentleman John Battles is a writer, painter, cartoonist, illustrator, songwriter, and archivist. His work has appeared in *Bad Trip*, *Black to Comm*, *Cool and Strange Music*, *Psychotronic*, and *Roctober Comics and Music*. An outsider solo musician, he has been performing his unique take on rockabilly and garage music for over twenty years. His heroes include Lester Bangs, Cub Koda, the Cramps, Wally Wood, Roky Erickson, and Frankenstein.

Jeremy Braddock is former editor and publisher of *Verbivore* magazine. He coedited, with Stephen Hock, *Directed by Allen Smithee* (University of Minnesota Press, 2001), a book of essays on Hollywood's fetish of the directorial pseudonym. He teaches and plays in bands in Philadelphia.

Ken Burke has been writing about music and musicians since 1985. His pieces have appeared in *Goldmine*, *Country Music Live*, *Blues Access*, *Country Standard Time*, *Roctober Comics and Music*, *Blue Suede News*, the *MusicHound Guides*, and the *Contemporary Musicians* series of books. He is the founder of the "Continuing Saga of Dr. Iguana" column. Burke currently resides in Black Canyon City, Arizona. Nobody knows why.

Nolan Dalla is a professional poker player and a full-time sports handicapper, and has been one of gambling's most respected writers for nearly a decade. He has written over 300 articles—published in *Card Player*, *Poker Digest*, *Gambling Times*, *The Intelligent Gambler*, *Western Gambler*, and other periodicals. Dalla created *Card Player* magazine's "Player of the Year" system, which rewards the top player in tournament poker. His odds on the World Series of Poker are also widely read. He is an instructor at "Poker School

Online" at www.PokerPages.com. Dalla is also currently the sports-handicapping columnist for *Casino Player* magazine. Dalla's daily report, along with gambling advice and sports-betting recommendations, can be found at www.madjacksports.com/nolan.htm. He lives in Las Vegas and is soon to release the biography of one of poker's most fascinating players, the late great Stu Ungar.

Greg Dinkin is the author of *The Poker MBA: Winning in Business No Matter What Cards You're Dealt* (www.thepokermba.com) and *Amarillo Slim in a World Full of Fat People* (with Amarillo Slim Preston). He is also the cofounder of Venture Literary (www.venture-literary.com), where he works with writers to find publishers for their books and producers for their screenplays. His essay originally appeared in *Card Player* magazine, where he is a featured columnist.

Robert Elder writes about film and pop culture for the *Chicago Tribune*. His work has also appeared in the *New York Times*, *Premiere*, *Gear*, Salon.com, the *L.A. Times* and the *Boston Globe*. A Montana native, Elder hangs his hat in Chicago.

Pete Fornatale is a writer and editor who lives in Brooklyn, New York. He has written two books about the 1980s: *Who Can It Be Now?* and *Say Anything*. His work has appeared in the *Washington Post* and *Maxim* and on playboy.com and espn.com.

Brett Forrest is the author of *Long Bomb: How the XFL Became TV's Biggest Fiasco* (Crown). His articles have appeared in *Spin*, Salon.com, *Rolling Stone*, *Men's Journal*, and the *New York Times Magazine*. He is currently working on several book projects in Moscow.

Jerome Gaynor published the comics anthologies *Bogus Dead* (2002) and *Flying Saucer Attack* (1995). Prior to that he produced his own comic zine, *Funkapotamus*. He spends most of his time hanging around with his four-year-old daughter, but he also makes Web sites, including the ridiculously popular www.stlpunk.com, which concerns his dual obsessions: punk rock music and St. Louis history. Look for information on his new comic project at www.jeromeempire.com.

Ira Glass is the host of *This American Life*, which is heard each week on over 400 public-radio stations. The show is produced by WBEZ Chicago and distributed by Public Radio International. Glass started playing poker after reading Jim McManus's blow-by-blow account of winning a quarter-million dollars in the World Series of Poker, as an amateur.

Carrie Golus has published two issues of the comic book *Alternator*, the second funded by a Xeric grant. She collaborates with her husband Patrick Welch on the comic-strip version of *Alternator*, as well as on illustrated non-fiction comics that have run in the newspaper *NewCity* and elsewhere. She is currently working on her first novel.

David Greenberger has been publishing *The Duplex Planet* since 1979 (www.duplexplanet.com). He lives outside Saratoga Springs, New York, with his wife and daughter. He is a regular commentator on National Public Radio.

Moira F. Harris is an art historian (Ph.D., University of Minnesota) with a research interest in popular culture. She has written about painted vehicles, outdoor murals and sculpture, Gambrinus, and the Hamm's bear. She is working on a book about the St. Paul Winter Carnival. She is also the publisher of Pogo Press, Incorporated, which publishes books concerning the arts, history, popular culture, breweriana, travel odysseys, and music. For a catalog or for further information, write to Pogo Press, Four Cardinal Lane, St. Paul, Minnesota 55127, or visit www.pogopress.com. An earlier version of her Coolidge article appeared in *Antiques and Collecting*.

Dave Hoekstra has been a *Chicago Sun-Times* staff writer since 1985. He is also a contributing writer to the *Chicago Reader* and *Playboy*. He won a 1987 Chicago Newspaper Guild Stick-O-Type Award for column writing, and his 2000 book *Ticket to Everywhere (The Best of the Detours Travel Column)* is available from Lake Claremont Press, Chicago. Hoekstra also coproduced *The Staple Singers: Chicago Stories*, a PBS documentary that was nominated for a 2001 Emmy Award. He lives in Chicago.

Dan Kelly lives in Chicago. His writings have appeared in *The Baffler*, *The Imp*, *The Rag-Time Ephemeralist*, and *Apocalypse Culture II*. He is a regular contributor to the *Chicago Journal*, for which he writes a semi-regular church review column. Mr. Kelly is studying the Korean martial art of hapkido, and he unashamedly enjoys playing guitar in an old-time string band with his wife Michael and friend Matt. His Web site is located at www.mrdankelly.com.

Starlee Kine is a producer for the Public Radio International show *This American Life*. She is currently in the market for a new poker club.

Karen Krizanovich is a writer, broadcaster, and columnist. Originally from Big Rock, Illinois, she now lives with her husband David Quantick in the middle of London. When it comes to cards, she is a terrible loser.

Ruth Lopez is a cultural journalist currently living in Chicago. She is the author of *Chocolate: The Nature of Indulgence* (Harry N. Abrams, Inc., 2002), published in conjunction with an exhibition originating at the Field Museum of Natural History. Lopez is a former fellow with the National Arts Journalism program at Columbia University.

Jason Lutes is a cartoonist and illustrator currently residing in Asheville, North Carolina. His published work includes the book *Jar of Fools* and the ongoing serialized comics novel *Berlin*.

Heather McAdams is a legendary underground cartoonist, underground animator, underground filmmaker, underground film instructor, and underground film archivist. She keeps her head above ground selling collectibles on eBay under seller name Recordroundup.

   Her brilliant and beautiful annual *Country Calendar* can be ordered by e-mailing Heather at Recordroundup@yahoo.com.

Richard Meltzer invented rock criticism (uh oh) and has written 10-11-12-13-14-15 books on a wide range of et cetera. Winner of the 2001 ASCAP-Deems Taylor Award for meritorious some such (or whatever), he is currently at work on a *very* filthy novel.

Eric Ottens lives in Chicago but pretends it's Tokyo. He spends his time playing with the Regal Standard band and seeking out talent for his site, www.themodernist.com. E-mail eric@themodernist.com.

Neal Pollack is the greatest living American writer, and the author of *The Neal Pollack Anthology of American Literature*. His first novel, a fictitious history of punk rock titled *Never Mind the Pollacks*, will be published this Fall by HarperCollins and will be accompanied by a genuine punk-rock album from his band, The Neal Pollack Invasion. He lives in Austin, Texas, with his family.

James Porter is a Chicago-based writer who, in addition to being a regular contributor to *Roctober Comics and Music* (since issue #3, 1992), has written for the *Chicago Sun-Times*, *Living Blues*, *No*

Depression, and *Blender*, and contributed several chapters to the book *Bubblegum Music Is the Naked Truth*, a history of bubblegum rock published by Feral House in 2001.

David Quantick is a comedy writer, music journalist, and radio and TV broadcaster. He has written books about music, contributed to many British comedy shows, and helped write Eddie Izzard's *Dress to Kill*. His favorite card game is blackjack, although he is so bad that people have left the table rather than play with him.

Elizabeth Rapoport is a freelance writer and editor. Her work has appeared in the *New York Times Magazine*, Salon.com, and *Redbook*, among others, and has been anthologized in *Mothers Who Think* and *Creme de la Femme*. She and the guys have been playing poker every Tuesday night for the last nine years; you'd think she'd be better.

Thomas Edward Shaw spent twenty years as a touring and recording musician, then started Carson Street Publishing in 1992. His books include *Cowboy Like Me* (Nevada-based short stories) and *black monk time* (a memoir of his years in the legendary garage band the Monks). His newest book, *Beltrami's River*, the creative narrative of an event that took place on the Mississippi River in 1823, was published in December, 2002. Shaw also publishes other writers. For more information, write to Carson Street Publishing, P.O. Box 5985, Reno, NV 89503, or send an e-mail to carsonstreet@gbis.com.

Tom Spurgeon is a writer living in Silver City, New Mexico. His latest project is a biography of longtime Marvel Comics spokesman Stan Lee, with media writer Jordan Raphael, for Chicago Review Press.

Jillian Steinberger turned down a proposal to elope to Vegas to be married at a drive-through Elvis church, and she's still single. A music journalist and culture reporter based in San Francisco, she writes for Amazon.com, *Bitch*, *Bust*, Neumu.net, *Punk Planet*, *Roctober Comics and Music*, and *Women Who Rock*.

Jacqueline Stewart, a childhood poker player, teaches at the University of Chicago.

Nikki Stewart is a Ph.D. candidate in women's studies at the University of Maryland. While she no longer plays poker, she enjoys computer solitaire on her study breaks.

Yuval Taylor hosts a biweekly poker game on Chicago's south side. Senior editor of Lawrence Hill Books and Chicago Review Press, his books include *I Was Born a Slave: An Anthology of Classic Slave Narratives*, *The Future of Jazz*, and *The Cartoon Music Book* (coedited with Daniel Goldmark).

Darrell Ticehurt is the founder and president of several successful software and Internet companies. He plays poker in his regular twice-weekly game, a game that has been played almost continuously since 1902, and he is considered a top-draw poker and hold 'em player. He is also known as an accomplished domino player, having won a number of major tournaments. A well-known big-game fisherman, he is on the board of Tournament Anglers Association, is a representative for the International Game Fish Association, and he fishes the Pacific Ocean out of Half Moon Bay, California. He writes a fishing column for *The Reel News*, a Seattle-based publication.

Waymon Timbsdayle writes music reviews for *Roctober Comics and Music* and apparently dabbles in poetry and poker.

Nick Tosches was born in Newark, New Jersey, and raised by wolves from the other side. His books include literate biographies of

Jerry Lee Lewis (*Hellfire*), Dean Martin (*Dino*), Sonny Liston (*The Devil and Sonny Liston*), and several novels, including the recent *In the Hand of Dante*. He has worked as a barroom porter, a snake hunter, a screenwriter, and a lyricist for a one-man band.

Chris Tsakis hosts a weekly phone-in talk show on WFMU (www.wfmu.org), and his commentaries have aired on NPR's *All Things Considered*. He wrote about Timothy Carey for the book, *OK, You Mugs: Writers on B-Movie Actors*. He's a resident of Hoboken, New Jersey. He'd love to get into a decent ongoing poker game.

Chris Ware was born in 1967 in Omaha, Nebraska. He is the author of *Jimmy Corrigan, the Smartest Kid on Earth* (Pantheon) and the ACME Novelty Library series of booklets and pamphlets (1993–present) and is the erstwhile editor of the music journal *The Rag-Time Ephemeralist*. He lives in Chicago with his wife Marnie; they have not reproduced.

Patrick W. Welch (The Painter of Hate™), as well as drawing non-fiction and fiction comics in collaboration with Carrie Golus, creates tiny narrative paintings. He is represented by Gescheidle in Chicago and Lyons Wier Gallery in New York. He teaches storytelling and drawing classes at the Illinois Institute of Art.

Bert Williams was a pioneer of African American humor and one of America's greatest entertainers. The Bert Williams homepage can be found at http://pubpages.unh.edu/~mgg/

David Wondrich is the author of *Esquire Drinks: An Opinionated and Irreverent Guide to Drinking* (Hearst, 2002) and *Stomp and Swerve: American Music Gets Hot, 1843–1924* (Chicago Review Press, 2003). He lives in Brooklyn.

Bill Zehme is a contributing editor for *Esquire* magazine, where his profile of Johnny Carson first appeared in June 2002. He is the author of the *New York Times* bestseller *The Way You Wear Your Hat: Frank Sinatra and the Lost Art of Livin'* and *Lost in the Funhouse: The Life and Mind of Andy Kaufman*. His most recent book, *Intimate Strangers: Comic Profiles and Indiscretions of the Very Famous*, collects twenty years of his renowned magazine journalism.